Praise fo
The Quarter-Life B

"Fresh and engaging, this book will inspire ~~the ~~ ~~~purpose."

—Tony Hsieh, CEO, Zappos.com;
New York Times bestselling author of *Delivering Happiness*

"I wish this book landed on my desk when I hit my quarter-life crisis! I could have saved years of frustration. Don't miss your own breakthrough; pick up this book!"

—Jon Acuff, *New York Times* bestselling author of *Do Over*

"With his triumphant *The Quarter-Life Breakthrough*, millennial Adam Smiley Poswolsky earns his place as a major voice of his generation. Pragmatic, philosophical, passionate, humble, delightfully funny, and infectiously inspiring, Poswolsky is a torchlight for those hungry to craft a more purposeful and rewarding adult life."

—Julie Lythcott-Haims,
New York Times bestselling author of *How to Raise an Adult*

"Smart stuff. Smiley moves past simplistic slogans and offers instead practical and nuanced strategies for succeeding in the noble task of crafting a working life that matters."

—Cal Newport, author of *Deep Work* and *So Good They Can't Ignore You*

"Smiley's words speak to the dreamer and doer in each of us by tapping into that true voice that calls from within."

—Elle Luna, artist; author of *The Crossroads of Should and Must*

"With clear stepping stones, *The Quarter-Life Breakthrough* is an honest and actionable guide for young people who are eager to see and seize meaningful opportunities."

—Tina Seelig, Professor of the Practice, Stanford University;
author of *What I Wish I Knew When I Was 20*

"Our generation never settles for careers they aren't passionate about. *The Quarter-Life Breakthrough* is the ultimate field guide to living life on your own terms and creating meaning in your work."

—Dan Schawbel, *New York Times* bestselling author of
Promote Yourself and *Me 2.0*

"This awesome book is chock full of smart, practical, relatable, and timely tips for meaning-makers. If you want to make a bigger impact in others' lives, connect with a community you love, and find greater fulfillment even in an ever-changing career landscape, buy this book. And then re-read it whenever you need to turn a breakdown into a breakthrough."

—Jenny Blake, author of *Pivot* and *Life After College*

"The *What Color Is Your Parachute?* for the millennial generation."

—Aaron Hurst, CEO, Imperative; author of *The Purpose Economy*

"I wish I had Smiley's voice in my head during my twenties. *The Quarter-Life Breakthrough* pairs the unvarnished reality with confident, simple exercises that will move you to act at just the right time."

—Dev Aujla, author of *Making Good*

The
QUARTER-LIFE
BREAKTHROUGH

Invent Your Own Path, Find Meaningful Work, and Build a Life That Matters

ADAM SMILEY POSWOLSKY

A TarcherPerigee Book

tarcherperigee

An imprint of Penguin Random House LLC
375 Hudson Street
New York, New York 10014

Most TarcherPerigee books are available at special quantity discounts for
bulk purchase for sales promotions, premiums, fund-raising, and educational needs.
Special books or book excerpts also can be created to fit specific needs. For details, write:
SpecialMarkets@penguinrandomhouse.com.

An excerpt from an early version of Chapter 1 appeared in "The career ladder
to nowhere" in *The Washington Post*, June 12, 2014.
An excerpt from an early version of the Introduction appeared in "4 Tips to Find
Meaningful Work" in *Fast Company*, April 16, 2014.
An excerpt from an early version of the Introduction and Chapter 4 appeared in
"How to Find Meaningful Work: Start With Asking the Right Questions"
in *GOOD*, April 13, 2014.

Library of Congress Cataloging-in-Publication Data

Names: Poswolsky, Smiley, author.
Title: The quarter-life breakthrough : invent your own path, find meaningful
work, and build a life that matters / Adam Smiley Poswolsky.
Description: First Edition. | New York, NY : TarcherPerigee, 2016.
Identifiers: LCCN 2016015566 | ISBN 9780143109525 (paperback)
Subjects: LCSH: Job hunting. | Career development. | Motivation (Psychology) |
BISAC: BUSINESS & ECONOMICS / Motivational. | BUSINESS & ECONOMICS /
Entrepreneurship. | BUSINESS & ECONOMICS / Careers / General.
Classification: LCC HF5382.7 .P685 2016 | DDC 650.1—dc23

Printed in the United States of America
1   3   5   7   9   10   8   6   4   2

Illustrations by Sumeet Banerji

This book is for anyone who ever heard,

"That's not possible, you can't do that, you're not good enough,

you don't have the qualifications, you're too young or too old,

you don't have the money or the connections, it's too late,"

and took a deep breath, *listened to their heart,*

and went out and did it anyway.

Sarah,
To your breakthrough!
With gratitude,
- SMILEY :)
3.22.17

CONTENTS

Introduction: My Quarter-Life Breakthrough   ix

PART ONE: INVENT YOUR OWN PATH   1

Chapter 1: Start Jumping Lily Pads   3
Chapter 2: No Mo' FOMO   17
Chapter 3: Embrace Fear   25

PART TWO: FIND MEANINGFUL WORK   35

Chapter 4: Define Meaningful Work   37
Chapter 5: Find Alignment   59
Chapter 6: The Infinite Paths to Meaningful Work   73
Chapter 7: How to Kick-Start Your Meaningful Job Search   93
Chapter 8: Is Graduate School Worth It?   116

PART THREE: BUILD A LIFE THAT MATTERS   125

Chapter 9: What to Do When Someone Tells You
    You're Not Ready for Your Dreams   127
Chapter 10: Get Your Breakthrough Hustle On   132
Chapter 11: Persistence Trumps Passion:
    Lessons in Breakthrough Hustling   150
Chapter 12: Find Believers   160
Chapter 13: Leave a Legacy   179
Conclusion: The Journey Continues   187

Join the Breakthrough Community   189
Gratitude   191
Bonus Gift   193

My Quarter-Life Breakthrough

*"How we spend our days is,
of course, how we spend our lives."*
—ANNIE DILLARD

HAVE YOU EVER known that you needed to make a change, but were completely unable to do anything about it? Have you ever felt like you were physically paralyzed by life, like you were trapped in a room and you couldn't get out?

That's exactly how I felt for almost two years at my job at the Peace Corps headquarters in Washington, DC. On paper and to the rest of the world, the job was perfect. I worked as the special assistant to the director of global operations and later was promoted to a program specialist. I got to sit in on senior staff meetings, draft important memos, and sometimes write remarks for the director of the Peace Corps. Once, I traveled to Botswana and worked with the Secret Service to help plan Michelle Obama's visit with Peace Corps volunteers.

The job had promotion potential. I was making $70,000 a year at the age of twenty-eight. I had the best health-care plan in the country, a matching 401(k) plan, and long-term job security.

My boss told me I was doing a great job, and that I was "indispensable" to the team. My parents were proud of me. When people at happy hour asked me the DC requisite *So, what do you do?* they were always impressed when I showed them my fancy business card and told them I worked at the Peace Corps.

Everything was perfect about my job, except for one tiny, very important thing: *I was miserable.*

Every time my alarm went off in the morning, I'd feel a shooting pain go up and down my back. I used to call this pain my "Morning Edition," because it coincided with NPR waking me up. *It's Morning Edition, for NPR News—I'm Steve Inskeep. And I'm Renée Montagne. Yesterday, the Senate blocked a measure to expand background checks for gun buyers and ban assault weapons, despite the recent tragedy at Sandy Hook Elementary School.*

My Morning Edition would shoot up and down my back when I was tying my tie before leaving the house, riding the bus down Sixteenth Street to work, and when I scanned my ID badge on the way in to the office. I'd feel it on the elevator ride upstairs, in weekly team meetings when we went over bullet-pointed to-do lists and discussed "best practices," and when I was out at a bar with friends, feeling my BlackBerry vibrate with an e-mail from my boss at ten p.m.

The pain, which manifested itself physically as shingles on my side (a stress-related nerve disease common among seventy-five-year-olds, not twenty-eight-year-olds), was actually far worse emotionally. It was the pain of knowing I wasn't where I was meant to be, but having no clue where I needed to go or how to get there. It was the pain of thinking something was wrong with me for having this great job that I wasn't energized by, a job that seemingly everyone else in my life was thrilled I had.

It was the pain of not being satisfied with working at the Peace Corps, a place that was making a positive impact in the world, whose mission was to promote world peace and friendship. I knew I wanted to help others, but if I wasn't happy at the *Peace Corps*, where the hell *would* I be satisfied working?

It was the fear that I might *never* make a change and be stuck forever in a job that wasn't right for me. It was the stress of not knowing the answers— what some people call a *quarter-life crisis*, although I certainly don't wish shingles upon the fifty million twentysomethings out there.

For over a year, I lived with my quarter-life crisis before I actually did anything about it. The experience was crippling. It was like my life was on hold. Being unhappy at work affected my ability to make simple decisions like what to eat for dinner or what to watch on Netflix. Every time I went to Target, I faced an existential crisis, because I didn't know whether I should buy a small or big bottle of shampoo, in case I decided to quit my job and move.

Receiving my monthly billing statement from Sallie Mae in my in-box made me want to throw my computer out the window. Looking at job postings on Idealist stressed me out because I had no idea what I was looking for. Seeing the covers of self-help books like *What Color is Your Parachute?*, *You Majored in What?*, and *Life's a Bitch and Then You Change Careers* overwhelmed me and made me nauseated.

I had a pile of career-change books that I kept zipped up in a suitcase in the back of my closet because it scared me so much just to look at them. At night, I scrolled through my Facebook news feed and saw all my friends' lives unfolding, and I was jealous: I wanted to be wherever they were, doing whatever they were doing.

I'd think to myself: Maybe *I* should move to Thailand? Maybe *I* should get my MBA? Maybe *I* should start my own nonprofit? Maybe *I* should work at a charter school? Maybe *I* should open my own food truck (even though I don't know how to cook, and I'm the world's worst driver). Maybe *I* should start an organic farm (even though I don't really like the smell of compost). Maybe *I* should get married and have kids (even though I don't even have a girlfriend!).

A friend of mine from college had already graduated from one of the top law schools in the country, gotten a job at one of New York City's top corporate law firms—making over $150,000 a year—and there he was on Instagram, traveling with his girlfriend in Peru, *proposing at sunset, in front of Machu Picchu*. I was like, *This* guy. He's already got a law degree and an amazing job, he's getting engaged to a beautiful woman—I hate my job, I hate my life, *I can't even get a date on OkCupid*, my life is ruined! I'm done for.

I'd lie in bed, unable to fall asleep. The choices besieged me. I felt helpless and alone.

It was only when I met other young people going through the same thing I was going through (minus the shingles) that I realized I wasn't alone in struggling to figure out what to do with my life, and felt empowered to have my breakthrough.

I wrote this book to prove it's okay to want something different from what you did two years ago. It's okay to leave a job everyone else thinks is awesome, and it's okay not to know exactly what it is you want at the age of twenty-two (or twenty-five or thirty or at any point). It's okay to invent your own path. In fact, you *have to* invent your own path. There is not one answer. Everyone is different, and you have to discover what works for you.

This is the book I wish I had during my own quarter-life crisis. This is the book I wish someone had handed to me when I graduated from college, headed to the same exact place I was before college (my parents' house). This book is about how a bunch of inspiring twenty- (and thirty-) somethings changed my life, and how their stories can help change your life, too.

WE'RE NOT THE "ME, ME, ME" GENERATION; WE'RE THE PURPOSE GENERATION

When I worked at the Peace Corps, I went to a free professional development class the office of personnel management was offering to employees from different government agencies. The class, called "Establishing a Business Mind-set," was held in a fluorescent-lit basement that smelled like chlorine, in an office building somewhere on K Street in downtown Washington, DC. The facilitator was at least sixty years old, bald and overweight, and wearing a wrinkled gray suit with dirty running shoes. He was chewing on a Subway sandwich when I arrived. This immediately threw me off—who eats Subway at nine o'clock in the morning?

At the beginning of the class, Mr. Subway asked each of us to introduce ourselves and say why we were there. There were about ten participants, and I was by far the youngest in the room. One woman answered that she was interested in starting her own Internet business on the side. I went next and said, "After I leave government, I'm interested in supporting entrepreneurs who are starting ventures that are making a social impact." When I mentioned the words "leave government," I could see the eyes rolling in the room, and hear someone clear their throat.

The guy who went after me said, "Well, this is a paid staff development day, so I don't have to be in the office, which means I'm one day closer to retirement." Of the people that followed, several had exactly the same answer. Another said, "I'm not at work, hallelujah."

I was surprised at how many people would attend a class about personal goal setting just to waste time, or check off another day in the long road toward their pension. But when you think about it, you can't blame them. This is how many of us are told to live our lives, either from our family or the media or even friends. This is the traditional "American Dream" retirement mind-set we learn from a young age: go to college, climb the ladder, find a well-paying job that allows you to support a family, retire at sixty-five, and you'll be fulfilled.

There's one slight problem with the retirement mind-set: it doesn't actually lead to fulfillment. Gallup's 2014 State of the American Workplace report showed that as many as 70 percent of American workers are disengaged at their jobs. Nearly one-fifth of those people were so disengaged at the office that they were *actively undermining* their coworkers' work. They were literally getting paid to screw things up for their company.

If you think it's crazy that millions of people spend their days unfulfilled, not showing up fully for themselves, their families, their companies, their communities, and the causes they believe in, you are not alone. Let me repeat that: *you are not alone.*

I think part of this lack of fulfillment stems from our failure as a society to encourage people to ask themselves simple questions that often don't yield simple answers: *Who am I? What do I want? What are my unique gifts? What do I want for the world? What types of people do I want to surround myself with? What is my purpose? Why am I here? Why?*

I've asked many of my peers *why?* over the last three years, and not once has someone answered, "make lots of money so I can buy nice stuff," "run a corporation so I can have lots of power," or "pass the time as quickly as possible, doing as little as possible, so I can retire with a pension in forty years and go on a cruise with my partner."

Rather, they've said things like: *I want to teach urban teenagers how to avoid debt and become successful entrepreneurs; I want to inspire young girls to think they can become engineers, and not Barbie dolls; I want to stop immigrants from getting wrongfully deported and separated from their families;* and *I want to empower all kids, regardless of what block they were born on, to reach their full potential.*

Young people aren't waiting for retirement. They're asking what their purpose is *now*, and they're determined to find the opportunities, organizations, and companies that share their dreams. Ninety percent of millennials want to use their skills for good, and a recent study by Net Impact showed that more than half of millennials would take a 15 percent pay cut to do work for an organization that matches their values. Deloitte's 2015 millennial survey found that nearly eight thousand future leaders from thirty countries think the business world is getting it wrong—some 75 percent say businesses are focused on their own agendas, rather than on improving society. In a popular *New York Times* op-ed titled "Millennial Searchers," Emily Esfahani Smith and Jennifer L. Aaker argued that "millennials appear to be more interested in lives defined by meaning than by what some would call happiness. They report being less focused on financial success than they are on making a difference."

In the next ten years, millennials (in this book, used to describe those born between 1980 and 2000) will make up 75 percent of the workforce. My generation is not alone in choosing meaning as more important than money in their lives. A recent study by IBM showed that Gen-Xers and Baby Boomers also rank meaning and purpose as a top factor in determining workplace engagement.

If the majority of the workforce expects to make a difference through their work, the important question becomes, how do you actually find meaning in the workplace? How do you find work that makes your heart sing, creates impact, and pays your rent? What are the tools and strategies that will help you be effective in achieving your purpose?

This book provides inspiring, honest, and counterintuitive career advice for anyone stuck in a quarter-life crisis (or third-life crisis, or midlife crisis—my mom is sixty-four and thinks she's having a quarter-life crisis) and figuring out what to do with their lives, from others who have recently gotten unstuck.

Regardless of where you're coming from, there are several assumptions I'm making about where you're going. If *any* of these assumptions apply to you, this book is for you.

First, **you refuse to settle for mediocrity**. You want to spend your days doing something that inspires you. You're less concerned with impressing your parents, your college professor, or your friends on Facebook, and more interested in pursuing the purpose that burns inside you. Instead of hearing someone else tell you you're successful, you'd rather discover what success means to you. You don't fit into a single box; you can't be defined by your college major, an acronym-prone personality test, a GMAT score, or one career path.

Second, **you want to make a positive difference in the lives of others**. Whether you want to solve a pressing social problem or make someone feel better about her day, you want to make an impact, you want to make a living doing something that matters. You want to dedicate your life to something greater than yourself.

And finally, **you're prepared to take action**. You know that the hardest part is starting the journey, but you're ready to begin making changes now. You want to come alive today—not when you're retired and sixty-five, but right now. You're willing to take baby steps now, to embrace being a lifelong learner now, to create self-care and wellness rituals now, to hustle now, to surround yourself with a community of believers now, to build a career that matters *right now*.

My friend Nate recently left his job to pursue his venture, The Loveumentary, a podcast and blog that shares stories about true love and healthy relationships. He explains his transition by saying, "I'd rather spend my days working on something I feel incredibly inspired by and proud of, than to waste them in a job counting down the minutes till I can go home. I decided that if I didn't like my life how it was, it was my job to change it, and so I did."

We spend nearly half our waking lives working. This book is for everyone who feels like Nate, who wants to reach their potential, spend their days working with purpose, and find meaningful work (as opposed to mediocre work).

Mediocre work is a job that pays the bills. It's something that passes the time, work you're not fully engaged with or interested in, for a cause or company that doesn't align with what you care about. Mediocre work may add to your financial well-being, but doesn't allow you to make your unique contribution to the world.

In contrast, this book contends that **meaningful work provides personal meaning, reflecting who you are and what your interests are; allows you to share your gifts to help others; provides a community of believers that will support your dreams; and is financially viable given your desired lifestyle.** I'll spend time later on in the book dissecting this definition and having you create a specific definition of what meaningful work is for you.

Viktor Frankl's best-selling and still-relevant book *Man's Search for Meaning* is about his experience in a Nazi concentration camp, during which he lost his pregnant wife and most of his family. Frankl wrote: "Being human always points, and is directed, to something or someone, other than oneself—be it a meaning to fulfill or another human being to encounter. The more one forgets himself—by giving himself to a cause to serve or another person to love—the more human he is."

Although there are multiple ways to define "meaning," I interpret Frankl's words to define meaning as something that comes not from personal gain, but from service or companionship, from positively impacting the lives of others.

Let's be real: it's hard enough for young people to find *any job* in today's job market. Finding meaningful work is even more challenging. According to the Pew Research Center, nearly half of American adults ages eighteen to twenty-four are jobless, the highest unemployment percentage since the government began collecting data sixty years ago. The US nonemployment rate among twenty-five- to thirty-four-year-olds (which includes the unemployed and those who have dropped out of the labor force) is over 25 percent.

Since 1983 (the year I was born), the average net worth of someone between the ages of twenty-nine and thirty-seven has fallen more than 20 percent. One in four adults between eighteen and thirty-four years old say they have moved back in with their parents after living on their own. Breaking from tradition, our generation may grow up to be *less* wealthy than our parents' generation.

Every generation probably feels like it has gotten the short end of the stick, but critics really love to hate on millennials. They call us the lazy generation, the entitled generation, and the "me, me, me generation." Based on the young people I know and the ones you'll read about in this book, these stereotypes couldn't be further from the truth. Millennials want to work—and despite being shackled by debt, recession, and the job crisis, they aren't motivated by money. Rather, they're driven to make the world more compassionate, innovative, and sustainable.

We aren't the "me, me, me generation." We are **the purpose generation**, and *we will be engaged with our work because we have to be.* The challenges facing our generation are simply too serious to ignore. They are too serious to only worry about on the weekends or after five p.m. We are a group of determined individuals who refuse to settle, because we know how great our impact can be when we find work we truly care about.

Most books and articles about twentysomethings focus on the *problem*: why we are doomed, in debt, depressed, lazy, unlucky, entitled, or addicted to Facebook. Instead, I am writing about the *solution*, so that anyone going through a quarter-life crisis can turn a moment of being stuck into a **breakthrough**, *a moment of opportunity and possibility when you discover why you're doing what you're doing and what you want to give to the world.*

As part of my journey over the last three years, I became a StartingBloc Fellow, completing a program that trains emerging leaders to drive social innovation across sectors and fosters a tight-knit community of change makers in fifty-five countries. I directed the Bold Academy, an intensive, residential leadership development program for young professionals interested in finding clarity, building confidence, and working with purpose. I also facilitated and ran community engagement efforts for the Hive Global Leaders Program, which has trained more than five hundred purpose-driven leaders and entrepreneurs from sixty countries, who are all working on creating a better world.

During this time, I've interviewed and met with hundreds of highly motivated millennials. Some of them quit their jobs to start their own ventures, some now work for the world's most innovative companies, and some are still figuring out the next step in their breakthroughs. My goal in capturing these stories was to discover *how we can each get a little bit closer to knowing why we're doing what we're doing and take action toward reaching our potential.*

In the summer of 2013, my own breakthrough swung into full gear, as I self-published the beta version of the book you're reading right now. Without much of a platform, and seeking to practice writing, I ran a crowdfunding campaign for the book, which raised nearly $13,000 from more than five hundred people in forty countries. It turned out that a lot of twentysomethings were struggling to find meaningful work, just like me.

When I told a friend that I was writing a book, he said, "I'm pretty sure that book has already been written like a hundred times, by people a lot smarter than you. You're just wasting your time."

I learned one important lesson early on in my journey: always ignore people who tell you not to pursue your dreams. Almost everything has already been done, but it hasn't been done by you, and that's all that matters.

In the spring of 2014, my self-published version of *The Quarter-Life Breakthrough* became a best-seller and the number one top-rated jobhunting book on Amazon, and paved the way for this book.

This book is a new and improved version of my self-published book. It shares inspiring stories of many twenty- and thirtysomethings who are figuring out how to work with purpose (and still pay their rent). It also tells my own story of how I escaped shingles and Facebook-induced FOMO ("fear of missing out"), grew my following from one subscriber (my mom), to several friends, to thousands of readers, and built a fulfilling (and financially sustainable) career around something I care deeply about: empowering my generation to pursue work that matters.

The goal of this book is to help you find purposeful work, work that makes you come alive and feel excited to start your day, even on a Monday morning (or at least *most* Monday mornings). Reading this book will help you get a little closer to who you are and discovering what your next step might be in the context of building a purposeful career.

That next step might be quitting your current job, finding a new job, changing jobs within your company, or embarking on an entirely new career path. It might be deciding whether to go to graduate school, pursue a side project you've been dreaming about, launch a crowdfunding campaign, or start your own business. The next step may seem small at first: experimenting with things that interest you, learning a new skill, and finding communities who will hold you accountable to your dreams. Or it might mean accepting that you don't know what the next step will be.

This book won't tell you what you should do with your life (how would I know? I've never even met you!).

It won't tell you to find "the perfect job" (how is it possible to know what your "perfect job" is before you've lived your life? What happens if the perfect job doesn't exist for you, but the *right* job does?).

It won't tell you to find your "true calling" (nobody has only one calling; even the so-called gurus who write books about finding your true calling have at least six callings—trust me).

It won't tell you to "quit your job, follow your passion, and live happily ever after" (we'll discover that this cliché is actually rather crappy career advice, and that most people who find meaning do not quit their jobs right away, but instead save money, invest in their skills, experiment with side projects, and hustle for months and sometimes even for years—while flirting with things that make them rather uncomfortable—in order to achieve their dreams).

It won't tell you to "do what you love" (we'll learn that most people who find meaningful work worry less about what they love, and more about their purpose, the unique contribution they can make to the world, and how they can *serve* the people they love).

And it won't tell you to work only four hours a week (why would you want to avoid something that might fulfill you? Why would you want to automate something that could give you joy? Why would you want to escape those who need your help?).

This book will simply empower you to get closer to finding a job or opportunity that allows you to share your gifts and make a positive impact in the lives of others. It will help you build a career—and a life—that matters.

Finding meaningful work is by no means easy, but it's not impossible, either. Unlike 70 percent of Americans, the millennials profiled in this book are excited about how they spend their days. They've done everything from teach fourth graders math to join the Foreign Service, leave a non-profit for a tech company, and leave a tech company for a nonprofit (and tons more in between). Any kind of work can be meaningful: the challenge is discovering *what in particular makes you come alive.*

Finding meaningful work requires asking many personal questions before it rewards any answers. Finding the work that makes you come alive is all about alignment and fit. What works for your friend may not work for you. You can have the wrong job at the right organization, or the right job at the wrong organization, or even the wrong job at the wrong organization.

Additionally, your purpose is constantly evolving as you learn new things, travel to new places, make new friends, start families, raise children, build communities, and grow older. What was purposeful for you one year may no longer be purposeful for you a few years later.

This book is divided into three parts, reflecting three stages in any quarter-life breakthrough.

In **Part One**, you'll start by taking small steps to invent your own path. I'll share the story of how I've had ten jobs since college, and argue that climbing a career ladder limits the potential for risk taking and experimentation, and is impractical in today's rapidly evolving and unstable job market. Instead of moving up and down on a ladder defined by someone else's version of success, we'll think of careers as a series of lily pads, extending in all directions, which allow you to jump to any new project or opportunity based on your purpose. You'll embrace the journey by moving beyond FOMO, listening when a light goes off telling you something isn't right, and using fear to guide you in the right direction.

In **Part Two**, you'll create your own definition of meaningful work. You'll discover how to align your work with your purpose and how to kick-start your job search by trying on jobs to see if they fit through short-term experiences and side projects. We'll talk about balancing money and meaning, and how to determine your breakthrough priorities. If graduate school is on your radar, we'll find out from several recent law school and business school graduates how to figure out whether grad school is "worth it" for you, and whether now is the right time for you to go back to school.

And finally, in **Part Three**, you'll get your breakthrough hustle on and take action toward getting what you want. You'll start by practicing self-love and prioritizing the things that make you happy. You'll do short exercises that will help you go outside your comfort zone and accomplish your goals. You'll brainstorm ways to invest in your breakthrough and build a supportive community of believers who share your values. Based on the stories of people like you who have recently had breakthroughs, you'll learn useful lessons in breakthrough hustling that will help you make an impact today and leave a legacy going forward.

An introduction wouldn't be complete without a few important caveats.

LIFE IS MORE THAN "WHAT YOU DO"

We live in a society that likes to define us by our job titles, how much money we make, who we know, and how cool our business cards look. While I lived in Washington, DC, I grew accustomed to answering the requisite *So, what do you do?* wherever I went. In fact, I once met a woman at happy hour who asked me for my business card before she even shook my hand or got my name—as if our interaction hinged on my job title.

I hated answering this question for a couple of reasons. First, because telling someone, "I'm the special assistant *to the* director of global operations at the US Peace Corps," kind of made me feel like Dwight Schrute talking to Michael Scott on *The Office*.

Second, because it didn't really describe who I was. It left out all the fun stuff—like the fact that my favorite thing to do in the world is sip green tea and write in my Moleskine, or that if it was up to me, I'd eat a bagel with lox and cream cheese every meal for the rest of my life, or that I have seen every single episode of *Seinfeld* fourteen times, and cannot have a conversation—even on a date—without busting into my Kramer voice (*"Oh, I'm stressed . . ."*).

Telling someone what I did for a living also didn't describe the people in my life who I love most. It left out my role model, my younger sister, who I talk to every day about life decisions as serious as whether she should go to law school and as trivial as whether it's appropriate for me to wear running shoes on an OkCupid date. My job title doesn't include how grateful I am for my friends, who make me laugh so hard I usually end up on the floor whenever I'm with them.

"What you do" matters—that's why you're reading this book—but life is more than a job. The time we spend outside the office, doing things we love with people we care about, is where many find fulfillment. However, since I'm thirty-two years old, live with five roommates in an apartment with an ant problem, recently attended a singles yoga class, and am still wearing running shoes and talking like Kramer on dates, I decided to write this book about something I can actually speak to: my journey over the last ten years to find meaningful work.

Having said that, I hope that some of the strategies to plan your break-through and become mindful about how you spend your days will bring you closer to the types of people and experiences that provide true joy and fulfillment, inside and outside the workplace.

MEANINGFUL WORK IS A RARE PRIVILEGE

Everyone deserves the chance to find meaningful work—*everyone*. However, the harsh reality is that most people wake up every day without the ability to decide what they do for a living. More than two billion people globally live on less than $2 a day. At least 1.2 billion people live in extreme poverty, lacking access to basic needs like clean drinking water, food, and sanitation services. Millions more—including in the United States, where 14.5 percent of the population (some forty-five million Americans) live below the poverty line—lack the financial ability, the access to education and health care, civil and human rights, or the physical freedom to make these choices.

Being able to choose what you do with your life is an enormous privilege, and it shouldn't be wasted. This doesn't mean that everyone who went to college and owns a MacBook should rush off to work in an impoverished African village, or that people with relative means are necessarily happier than people without (some research suggests otherwise). But it does mean that those of us fortunate enough to decide what we do should think deeply about what we care about, how we want to use the time we have, and how we can each leave this world a little better than we found it.

My friend Nikita Mitchell put it far better than I can. Nikita graduated from UC Berkeley's Haas School of Business, where she became the first black woman ever to serve as president of the school's MBA Association. Passionate about diversity and gender issues, Nikita was concerned that her business school class was only 29 percent women (and that she was one of only three black women in the entire class). Nikita and a group of her classmates launched an effort to work with the Haas administration and admissions office to recruit more women MBAs, and in just one year, helped increase the percentage of women in Haas's first-year MBA class to 43 percent, making it the business school with one of the largest percentages of female students in the country. And it didn't stop there. They ultimately created an initiative that has since been passed down to new student leaders, outlining a vision for creating a more inclusive culture for women who attend business school.

"It is the greatest gift to be able to stop and think about what you want," Nikita told me. "It is the epitome of privilege. You have to have the money, the resources, and the time that most people in this world just don't have. When you've been given that kind of privilege, and you've been given the kind of education I've been given, the kind of resources I've been given, it would basically be throwing away all of the sacrifices that my parents made to come to this country, to put me through school, all of the things that my ancestors have fought for—if I didn't stop and think about what matters to me and what I should contribute to the world."

ALL WORK CAN BE MEANINGFUL

There is a widespread misconception that only certain jobs are meaningful—the types of jobs you read about in business self-help books like this one—jobs in fields like social entrepreneurship, tech, poverty alleviation, health care, education, media, and the arts. The truth is that *any job* can be meaningful. *Any job, however unfulfilling to you, might be incredibly meaningful to someone else.*

During one of my first speaking engagements about how to find meaningful work, I made a comment I now regret. I said, "Millennials like me don't want to work for meaningless apps that help rich people get their laundry done faster; they want to work for companies that actually change the world." I had just read an article by George Packer in *The New Yorker*, who was lambasting Silicon Valley, astutely observing that "the hottest tech start-ups are solving all the problems of being twenty years old, with cash on hand, because that's who thinks them up." I made my comment because I believe my generation is actually looking beyond making on-demand delivery apps for wealthy people, and instead using our careers to make a deeper social impact.

I no longer make that comment, and here's why. At a speaking engagement a few months later, a man named Nicholas Sanderson came up to me and told me about Laundry Locker, a ten-year-old laundry and dry cleaning business he now runs in San Francisco. Laundry Locker allows people to drop off their dry cleaning and laundry in lockers, and then cleans it for them while they are at work. Nicholas told me that many of the individuals he employs come from troubled backgrounds and have had a hard time finding traditional employment. What he finds meaningful is providing them with a stepping-stone toward something bigger and better in their careers. These passionate individuals can learn transferable skills and relationship development tactics that make them employable for their next big roles, which in turn is meaningful to them and their families.

Never (ever) assume that your work is more meaningful than someone else's. Everyone is different, and all work can be meaningful; the challenge is finding what's meaningful to you.

READING THIS BOOK IS JUST THE BEGINNING

The last time I picked up a career-change book, I put it down after two minutes and hid it in my closet. That terrifying book was 373 pages long, packed with intimidating goal charts and worksheets that looked like something from the SAT, and full of statistics and case studies of how famous, rich people like Bill Gates and Mark Zuckerberg started their careers.

Instead of writing a book like the one I hid in my closet, I decided to write a short book without too many statistics, but with a lot of fun exercises, helpful resources, and engaging stories of young people figuring out what to do with their lives. Here's how to get the most out of this book:

- **Do the exercises.** Throughout the book you'll find practical exercises and reflections intended to help you at each stage of your breakthrough. These are meant to be fun, useful, and as un-SAT as possible. You may find it helpful to have a journal or sketchbook close by, in case you want to jot down any ideas. If some of the exercises don't work for you, skip them. Come back to them later (just don't hide this book in your closet!).
- **Share your story.** The gifted twenty- and thirtysomethings whose stories I tell didn't start companies like Microsoft and Facebook. They're not famous, and they're definitely not rich. They're my friends, whom I love and who have inspired me to dream bigger. All of them are still figuring it out, like you and me. Each has failed and succeeded in some way or another. By the end of this book, I hope you'll share your own narrative of what you want for the world, just like my friends did.

Everyone is different. There is no right answer or cure-all when it comes to finding meaningful work. The people who find it are the ones who spend time looking for it. *The only person who knows what is right for you is you.* No self-help author (especially one nicknamed "Smiley"), career counselor, life coach, parent, boss, acronym-prone personality test, GRE, LSAT, or GMAT score, or friend's Facebook post can start making these decisions for you.

You have to start sometime, so how about right now?

PART ONE

Invent Your Own Path

PART ONE

CHAPTER 1

Start Jumping Lily Pads

"Not all those who wander are lost."
—J. R. R. TOLKIEN

TAPED ABOVE MY desk is an article from the Onion with the headline "24-Year-Old Receives Sage Counsel from Venerable 27-Year-Old," and a picture of two twentysomethings in plaid shirts in deep existential conversation over pints of beer at a bar.

When I told my dad I was writing a career advice book, he looked at me like I was crazy and asked, "What qualifies *you* to be writing a book about careers? You've changed what you wanted to do with your life every other year since you were a kid."

My dad is absolutely right. I've never been able to focus on any one thing for very long, and I still have trouble answering the question "What do you want to be when you grow up?" At first, I wanted to be Big Bird, road-tripping around the country in *Follow That Bird*. Then I wanted to be Mister Rogers. Once, my family was staying at a hotel, and Fred Rogers was there having breakfast. I ran right up to him and exclaimed, "Excuse me, Mister Rogers, Mister Rogers! How did you get out of the TV?!"

When I was in fourth grade, I wanted to be a play-by-play announcer for the Olympics. In eighth grade, I wanted to be Adam Sandler. In high school, I wanted to be a sports writer. Then I went to a liberal arts college, which is to say I majored in film studies, studied abroad in Cuba, and took intro to dance senior year. Making career choices has proved difficult ever since.

After graduation, I could write a fifteen-page shot-by-shot analysis of David Lynch's *Mulholland Drive* and tell you the difference between cage-free, free-range, and pasture-raised eggs. But I realized that college had not prepared me for the job-finding process in the slightest. Since I had no idea

3

which "career ladder" to climb, I moved to the city where all my friends were moving (Brooklyn), and got a job that matched my college major (film), which is what I thought I was supposed to do at the time.

In the ten years since graduation, I've had ten drastically different jobs, lived in six cities, and gone down four career paths. I've never once seen this elusive "career ladder" everyone talks about. But I do know that whoever invented the ladder has been freaking twentysomethings out for a long time.

Where do you get on the ladder? Is there one in each city in the world? If you hop off for a detour, do you have to start back from the bottom, or do you get to keep your place in line? Is there music along the way? Is it like Pandora—can I choose my station?

As insufferable as this ladder mind-set can be, twentysomethings are still unfailingly being told to maintain a linear career trajectory. Even my father, who was born in the 1950s, hasn't followed any sort of career path. He has worked in stage management and lighting design for off-off-Broadway shows, then for a rock 'n' roll theater start-up in London, dropped out of NYU's theater school, sailed across the Atlantic, joined Pink Floyd as a roadie doing lighting on their international tours, became disenchanted with life on the road and enrolled in architecture school, worked as an architect, raised kids, spent time in corporate real estate, got his MBA at the age of fifty-three, built dialysis clinics, and managed projects and workplace innovation for a large electronics company. Yet even he was skeptical when I told him I wasn't pursuing a "traditional" career path after college, and instead was headed to New York to freelance on film sets.

If you've struggled with picking a career path, or focusing on one interest or calling, then you're not alone. Only 27 percent of college graduates have a job related to their college major.

In high school and during college, I scooped ice cream at Ben & Jerry's, had a few stints as a barista, and among other things, worked at a garden shop, helping customers pick out shade perennials (pretending that I actually knew what a shade perennial was). To list all of my high school and college jobs would be overwhelming. Here's the eclectic array of jobs I've held since graduating from college.

MY WANDERING JOURNEY

Age   Job + Motivation

18   **Student at Wesleyan University** *(Middletown, CT)*
       Make friends, protest George W. Bush, gain liberal arts education

22   **Move back home with parents** *(Cambridge, MA)*
       Unemployed and broke

22   **Freelance film location scout** *(Brooklyn, NY)*
       Live with best friends in Brooklyn, major in film, love movies

25   **Film festival assistant** *(Buenos Aires, Argentina)*
       Live in Argentina, learn Spanish, travel

26   **Obama 2008 campaign field organizer** *(Anderson, IN)*
       *Join change movement, support gay marriage, keep John McCain
       from destroying the world*

26   **Waiter at Eatonville restaurant** *(Washington, DC)*
       Make money to pay rent, love food and people

27   **Move back home with parents** *(Cambridge, MA)*
       Unemployed and broke

27   **Special assistant at US Peace Corps** *(Washington, DC)*
       *Believe in Peace Corps' mission to promote world peace and friend-
       ship*

30   **Freelance writer & Bold Academy director** *(San Francisco, CA)*
       Live in San Francisco, love to write, support social entrepreneurs

32   **Author, speaker, and Hive Global Leaders Program facilitator**
       (San Francisco, CA)
       *Empower millennials to have breakthroughs and find meaningful
       work*

There are two mind-sets through which one could analyze my "career" up to this point. The first is what I'll call the **career ladder mind-set**, the one we've been taught to follow most of our lives. This mind-set tells us that the more AP classes we take, the better we do on our SATs, the better college we go to, the more money we make, the higher on the ladder we rise, the more successful we are.

Someone with this mind-set would look at my career and say, "This kid Smiley is a hot mess; he lived at his parents' house at the age of twenty-seven! He can't make up his mind. He won't stay in a job for more than two years. He'll never be successful because he's not on a specific career ladder. Think of where he could have been if he had spent the last eight years in film."

Although recent college graduates are often encouraged to adopt a career ladder mind-set, these career ladders have several essential flaws:

- **Career ladders limit new opportunities, experimentation, and risk taking.** What happens if an amazing opportunity presents itself—say, to join the 2008 Obama campaign—and I want to get off the ladder, but I've already spent two years on a different career? Ladders encourage people to avoid new challenges in exchange for safety and "moving up." Avoiding these risks may mean avoiding the very opportunities that provide us the greatest satisfaction in life. If there isn't only one answer, there probably isn't one "top of the ladder," either.
- **Career ladders define success on someone else's terms.** Career ladders lead to promotion potential and higher salary. The theory is, "Pay your dues early, and you'll reap the benefits later." I'm not a huge fan of delayed gratification in general—not many millennials are—but it's especially annoying when I don't even get to define what my gratification is or what success means to me. What happens if I'm not in it for a fancy job title or a big salary? What happens if success for me is not my retirement package at sixty-five, but one person realizing their life potential from a book I write?
- **Career ladders make me stress about the future, which inhibits me from taking action now.** When I was thinking about leaving my job

at the Peace Corps, one of the things I was interested in pursuing next was writing. Whenever I brought up the possibility of becoming a freelance writer, all I heard from people was, "Well, it's a hard career ladder to climb. You can't get a staff writing position at a major newspaper anymore. Newspapers don't even exist. *The New Yorker* receives one hundred thousand submissions an hour."

To some degree, the people warning me not to go into freelance writing at the age of twenty-eight were right: writing is extremely competitive, and it's the opposite of financially lucrative. But stressing about my future career as a writer and about where I'd end up ten or twenty years down the road *nearly stopped me from even trying*. I hadn't even written a blog post yet, and I was thinking about writing for *The New Yorker*. I was stressing about the future, instead of taking action now.

The best advice I got about starting a writing career was from my friend Ryan Goldberg, a freelance journalist who lives in Brooklyn and has numerous bylines in *The New York Times*. At the time we talked, Ryan was also refereeing dodgeball to supplement his income. He told me, "Smiley, if you want to be a writer, write. Start writing today."

STOP CLIMBING LADDERS, START JUMPING LILY PADS

The other way of looking at my career is through what I'll call the **lily pad career mind-set**. My friend and career strategist Nathaniel Koloc sometimes describes careers as a series of lily pads, extending in all directions. Each lily pad is a job or opportunity that's available, and you can jump in any direction that makes sense for you, given your purpose (how you want to help the world). Nathaniel founded ReWork, a talent firm that places purpose-seeking professionals in social impact jobs, and then served as director of talent for Hillary Clinton's 2016 presidential campaign. He has made it his job to study how people build careers worth having.

Nathaniel says, "There is no clear way 'up' anymore—it's just a series of projects or jobs, one after another. You can move in any direction; the only question is how you're devising your strategy of where to move and where you can 'land,' i.e., what you're competitive for."

Leaping to another lily pad for a new job or opportunity doesn't mean you're going backward. There is no backward. You can't go backward if you're learning. The lily pad career mind-set argues that motivated people who want to align their work with their purpose *should consider frequent small career jumps based on their changing purpose and interests*. This is especially important in a difficult job market that requires job seekers to constantly evolve and develop new skills to remain competitive.

Which of the following scenarios inspires you to take action?

1. Spending ten to twenty years going in one specific direction, climbing a ladder until someone else tells you that you are "successful."
2. Spending ten to twenty years exploring multiple lily pads, learning and experimenting as you go, seeking fulfillment as defined by the unique contribution you want to make.

Leaping between lily pads means you're getting closer to wherever your roots, your interests, and your learning desires are pulling you. Motivated people who want to align their work with their purpose should embrace flexibility and experimentation when it comes to their careers. This doesn't mean that you have to quit your job every two years, but it does mean that you have to consistently check in to see if what you're working on excites you or is making a valuable contribution.

Instead of one ladder leading straight up, the **lily pad career mind-set** visualizes your career as a pond of lily pads, a series of interconnecting leaps you've made between different opportunities. What's holding everything together is the roots: what you care about and how you want to help the world. In my case, today my roots are driving me to inspire others through writing, speaking, and helping others to realize their full potential. Your roots may be driving you to do one thing now, but that thing may change in five years.

Your education doesn't stop when you graduate from college; in fact, a whole new aspect of it begins the day you enter the workforce. Rather than simply checking a box for your major at the age of twenty, when you barely know what your university has to offer (let alone what life has to offer), accept that you're going to be a lifelong learner. Instead of climbing a career ladder that might not be around in five or ten years, treat your career like a lifelong experiment. Every job, every experience, every place you travel, is a chance to learn something new about yourself, what interests you (and, importantly, what doesn't), what you're good at, and what type of impact you want to have on the world.

Our new economy is characterized by rapid technological innovation. How we communicate and how we work are constantly changing in an increasingly global job market. The US Department of Labor has noted that 65 percent of today's grade school kids will end up in jobs that haven't been invented yet. Whether they want to or not, fewer and fewer people are staying in one job for a long period of time. According to the Bureau of Labor Statistics, in 2014 the median job tenure for twenty- to twenty-four-year-olds was less than 1.5 years, for twenty-five- to thirty-four-year-olds it was only three years, and for all workers twenty-five and over it was 5.5 years. If the majority of millennials are staying in their jobs for less than three years, that means some will have four jobs by the age of thirty, and as many as fifteen to twenty jobs in their lifetime.

In an article about "generation flux" and how to succeed in this new business climate, Robert Safian, editor of *Fast Company*, argues that we need a mind-set that embraces instability and recalibrating careers. "Our institutions are out of date," he writes. "The long career is dead; any quest for solid rules is pointless, since we will be constantly rethinking them; you can't rely on an established business model or a corporate ladder to point your way; silos between industries are breaking down; anything settled is vulnerable."

PAY ATTENTION WHEN YOUR PURPOSE CHANGES

The story of my friend Ryan Allis teaches us that it's never too late to adopt a lily pad career mind-set. Ryan became an entrepreneur at the age of eleven when his family moved to Bradenton, Florida, where a large percentage of the neighbors were over the age of sixty-five. Ryan's Uncle Steve sent him one of his old Macintosh computers, and Ryan learned everything he could about the computer, played SimCity for hours, and read *PC World* cover to cover. He felt as ready as an eleven-year-old could ever be, so he created a flyer that said, "Need computer help? For $5 an hour, a responsible eleven-year-old will come to your house. Call Ryan." His parents even let him get his own landline number to advertise on the flyers, which he posted around the neighborhood, at the library, at the laundromat, at city hall, and in people's mailboxes.

Ryan's first call wasn't from a potential customer, it was from the local postmaster, who asked to speak to his parents. The postmaster general was upset at Ryan's mom for letting her son put flyers in mailboxes without paying for stamps. "That was the first important lesson I learned about entrepreneurship: sometimes you have to act first and ask permission later," recalls Ryan. "It's okay to push the boundaries a little bit."

A few weeks later, Ryan made his first sale. He rode his bike to help an older man named Jim with his computer for an hour. Jim paid him $10 (double his rate), and then told his buddies at the bingo hall about Ryan. Soon Ryan was receiving lots of calls from other senior citizens in the neighborhood, and he began showing them how to set up AOL and send pictures to their grandchildren. Ryan made $400 that summer before seventh grade, and by the end of high school he was making $1,000 a month as a freelance web designer.

As a freshman at UNC Chapel Hill, Ryan met a senior computer science major named Aaron Houghton, who was developing a product that would help small businesses manage their contact lists and send e-mail newsletters. Aaron and Ryan joined forces to build an e-mail marketing software company, with Aaron developing the software and Ryan handling the marketing and acquiring customers. They named their company IntelliContact Pro, which later would become iContact, and spent the first years bootstrapping the company, not paying themselves a salary, and surviving off ramen noodles, Hot Pockets, and $1.99 subs.

In order to focus all his energy on building iContact, Ryan dropped out of college, becoming a CEO at the age of eighteen. He wrote in his journal,

I just know that I do not want to be normal. I do not want to be the guy that after four years of college has trouble finding a job because of the job market. I have knowledge right now that will make me never have to rely on the job market. I do not want to be stuck in the rat race my entire life. I think now I have a chance to get out.

By the end of 2003, using search engine optimization and affiliate marketing to grow their client base, Ryan and Aaron had four full-time employees and seventy-eight paying customers. That year, iContact earned $12,000 in revenue. The following year, they made $300,000. By 2006, Ryan and Aaron had grown iContact to $1.5 million in sales and raised $500,000 of venture capital. Several years later, iContact did $50 million in sales and had three hundred employees.

Ryan had achieved a level of success in his twenties that most entrepreneurs only dream of. But was he fulfilled? Not if you take into account his health. While growing iContact, Ryan was living out of his office, working day and night. He was overweight, surviving on a diet of fast food and Keurig instant coffee, and getting little sleep. He had heartburn and frequent anxiety attacks.

In 2008, Ryan's priorities started to shift. He visited his friend's start-up Village Energy, in Kampala, Uganda, where he met people living on less than $1.25 a day. He recalled a journal entry he had written a few years earlier: *Am I spending my time in a worthwhile manner? I am really passionate about development economics and ending poverty and hunger. Much more so than I am about e-mail marketing. I can make positive social change through business and through iContact, but is it enough? Probably the biggest recurring tension in my life right now is the struggle between wanting to build iContact over the next three years and realizing how great of an opportunity it is, and knowing deep down I am not yet fully aligning what I love with what I do. I am enjoying building iContact, have wonderful people around me, and am learning tons. But I know something is missing.*

At the end of 2011, when his mom was diagnosed with a brain tumor at the age of fifty-nine, Ryan did everything he could to help her as her tumor grew from the size of a pea to that of a tennis ball. Knowing that his mom would have the best chance of survival if the most qualified surgeon in Tampa, Florida, performed the operation, Ryan tried to make an appointment for his mom. The specialist had a six-month waiting list. Undeterred, Ryan did everything possible to save his mom's life, calling nearly fifty people in twenty-four hours to see if they could help get his mom to see the best doctor available. Through his efforts, Ryan discovered that his ex-girlfriend's father was the former governor of Florida. The former governor made a call to the hospital and Ryan's mom was admitted.

Sadly, Ryan's mother passed away from cancer, but Ryan learned an important life lesson: anything is possible when you're aligned with your mission. Ryan accepted that his mission was something other than building e-mail marketing software. The following year, iContact was sold to Vocus for $170 million.

Several years after his breakthrough, a lot has changed in Ryan's life. His new mission is to unlock human potential and create a world without poverty, where everyone has access to basic needs, and where as many people as possible are self-actualized. Ryan moved to San Francisco, where he's now chairman of Hive, which trains purpose-driven entrepreneurs and leaders to create an abundant, sustainable, and joyous world for all people. He used to think yoga was something middle-aged women did after pregnancy to get back in shape, but today he practices yoga and meditates every day. Yoga has helped reduce the chronic neck pain he's had since a car crash in high school. Ryan has changed his diet from instant coffee, Hot Pockets, and potato chips to healthier foods like kale, quinoa, avocados, and nuts and fruit, which has helped him to lose sixty pounds, avoid heartburn, and not have an anxiety attack in four years.

When Ryan got to the top of the career ladder, he realized it was someplace he didn't even want to be. Instead of climbing the ladder to nowhere, he's now building a career that matters to him. He made a decision based on his own priorities (not on what another tech entrepreneur would say) and ignored the misconception that career choices have to be linear (he went from building e-mail marketing software to running a leadership development program).

People change. So should what they do for a living. "I became a tech entrepreneur at the age of eleven, when my uncle gave me that computer," recalls

Ryan. "And I woke up at the age of thirty, and I was still a tech entrepreneur. But I had never actually asked myself, 'Am I a tech entrepreneur because I actually want to be? Is this what truly brings me alive?'"

LEARN YOUR PURPOSE

While he'll always be skilled in technology, Ryan is now focused on developing his gifts for building community and coaching leaders. Ryan's story proves that nobody has only one life purpose. But you still need to have a purpose, maybe not *the* purpose, but *a* purpose, a mission that fuels how you spend your days. For most of his youth, Ryan's mission was building technology and making money. Today, Ryan is wealthy enough that he no longer needs to work. Many people in his shoes would probably buy a yacht, sail around the world, and find a beach somewhere in the Caribbean to pass the days drinking piña coladas. Not Ryan. Ryan is hustling harder than ever before, because he is dedicated to a new purpose: being an authentic leader who inspires others to create a more abundant, sustainable, and joyous world for all people.

During Hive, Ryan leads participants through a life purpose exercise in which he shares a slide about what it means to be an authentic leader. An authentic leader, Ryan argues, *has aligned their personal purpose with their professional purpose.* An inauthentic leader is tense when they wake up in the morning, because they spend their day doing something they don't care deeply about. An authentic leader can barely wait to wake up in the morning, because they're so excited to work on their mission, and inspire others to work on it, too.

If you're not sure what your purpose is right now, I don't recommend going on a road trip around the world to read lots of self-help books and "find yourself." You're just going to waste lots of money on gas, become even more confused, and probably end up wanting to renounce all your material possessions and move to Thailand (yes, this happened to a friend of mine).

If you're not sure what your purpose is now, I recommend that you do what Ryan did. Instead of trying to *find* your purpose, *learn your purpose.*

Take action. Explore your talents. Pay attention to what you see and how it makes you feel. Pay attention when your motivations start to change. Don't be afraid to try new things. Be willing to reinvent yourself, even if that means evolving from a workaholic tech entrepreneur so obsessed with affiliate marketing that he sleeps on the floor of his office, to a California yogi who eats lots of kale and wants to save the world. Anything is possible if you are bold enough to learn your own life's mission.

Ryan's story reminds us that there is not only one answer, and we have to be willing to explore multiple answers. This doesn't mean you have to change jobs or move cities every other year (you may find that your breakthrough brings you somewhere you stay for many years, or even your entire career), but it does mean you'll have to frequently *consider* your changing purpose and interests, to get closer to what you want for yourself and the world.

The journey is the journey—there is no finish line, no top of the ladder. Your career is simply a series of journeys. Some may be tiny pivots. Others may be huge leaps to new lily pads. Embrace this journey that you're on today. As my friend and yoga teacher Julia Winston reminds me, "We run forward, we push, we have goals, we dream, to get to the present." (No, Julia is not my singles yoga teacher. That guy doesn't talk about the journey, he plays Marvin Gaye's "Let's Get It On" during savasana.)

CAREER EXPERIMENTATION IS NOT QUITTING YOUR JOB TO CHILL ON THE BEACH

What's the difference between career experimentation and wasting time? I know they can look eerily similar sometimes. I didn't write this book so young people could avoid worrying about the future. I wrote it so they could feel empowered to *take tangible steps right now toward working with purpose.*

There's an excellent TED talk called "Why Thirty Is Not the New Twenty," by clinical psychologist Meg Jay, author of *The Defining Decade: Why Your Twenties Matter—And How to Make the Most of Them Now.* The book is based on her work with numerous young people experiencing quarter-life crises. In her book and TED talk, she argues that one of the reasons that half of all twentysomethings are unemployed or underemployed is that many avoid taking their twenties seriously. Because they put off important decisions about personal identity, career, and family, they end up facing more serious life crises when they're older.

I agree—at least about the personal identity and career part. I can't really speak about settling down and raising a family yet, since I'm still going to singles yoga. *The time for intentional learning, experimentation, and action is now.*

The lily pad career mind-set doesn't say "your twenties don't matter," or "don't worry about your career until you're older." On the contrary, I'm advocating that you take advantage of opportunities when they present themselves, and thoroughly explore different career options to get closer to who you are, what you value, and how you want to help others.

What sense would it have made for me to stay in government if I was tired of working in government, just to wait for retirement in thirty-five years? None. Just like it would have made no sense for Ryan to keep sleeping in his office, eating Hot Pockets, and selling e-mail marketing software, when he was ready to empower purpose-driven leaders.

Build a purposeful career by experimenting with opportunities you actually care about. This isn't wasting your twenties or thirties—it's making them count.

Breakthrough Exercise: Life Storytelling

On the first day of the Hive Global Leaders Program, participants from thirty countries around the world share a five-minute version of their life story. It takes me an hour to explain my trip to the store to buy a bottle of kombucha, so telling my entire life story in five minutes is definitely a challenge. However, the time constraint is designed to make participants focus on the most important moments of their life, the moments of tension and transition that have influenced their journey. Hearing another person's life story is far more powerful than knowing their résumé and all the places they've worked. When you know someone's life story, you get closer to knowing *why* they're here.

Being able to articulate the defining moments that have shaped your life will help you get closer to realizing who you are and what your breakthrough is all about. If you don't have someone to share with, try writing your life story down on a piece of paper for five minutes, identifying the two or three moments in your life that have had the most impact on your journey so far. Examples of these moments might include where you grew up, the death of a family member or close friend, your college experience, traveling to a foreign country, quitting your job, falling in love, falling out of love, or even reading your favorite book.

BREAKTHROUGH TAKEAWAYS

- The career ladder is an outdated metaphor that is not practical in today's job market. Today's evolving job market rewards those with a wide range of skills and experiences, who are curious, resourceful, and inventive.
- The lily pad career mind-set argues that motivated people who want to align their work with their purpose should consider frequent small career jumps based on their changing purpose and interests.

If you're not sure what your purpose is now, learn it. Take action. Explore your talents and interests. Take small steps right now toward working with purpose.

CHAPTER 2

No Mo' FOMO

"If I didn't define myself for myself, I would be crunched into other people's fantasies for me and eaten alive."
—AUDRE LORDE

DURING MY QUARTER-LIFE crisis (shingles and all), I felt paralyzed, unable to make a change. I felt like I was at the intersection of hopeless, stuck, and FOMO ("fear of missing out").

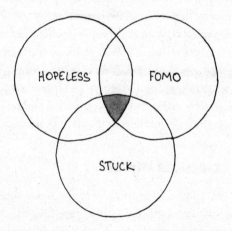

I told myself the following:

I'm hopeless: "I wish I could do _____. But that's impossible; I'd never be able to do that. There're no jobs available in that field. It would take years to do that. It's too late to do that—I'm already twenty-eight."

I'm overdosing on FOMO: "All my friends on Facebook are so happy and successful. I'm so jealous. I want to do what they're doing. Some of my friends are lawyers now—that's nuts! A kid I went to college with was nominated for an Oscar! My friend started a company, and he's a *Forbes* 30 Under 30. Wow, my buddy is traveling around Southeast Asia. I feel so boring. Everyone is getting engaged—I'm tired of being single."

I'm stuck: "I hate my job. I want to do something else, but I don't know where to start. I'm interested in so many things, but none of them seems perfect. There are too many choices of what I could do next. I'm overwhelmed, stressed, and all I want to do is watch *Mad Men*. Or maybe *Game of Thrones*. I can't even decide which *TV show* to watch."

Everything feels impossible during a quarter-life crisis, even small decisions like which size shampoo to buy or which TV show to watch. But to truly embrace the journey means you need to truly change your perspective, from helplessness to possibility.

In this chapter, you'll learn three easy steps to adopt a **breakthrough perspective**, a perspective that says: *rather than feel like everything is impossible, I'm going to take tangible steps and start exploring what I'm interested in.*

If you're feeling hopeless, full of FOMO, stuck, or any combination of those three, there are some clear ways to begin changing your perspective: express gratitude, stop comparing yourself to others, and listen to your true self. Having a breakthrough perspective will help you start exploring your interests so you can jump to the next lily pad in your journey toward meaningful work.

HOPELESS → EXPRESS GRATITUDE

I learned about what really matters in life from my grandmother. Gran grew up during the Depression, when her family lost everything they had. She learned to take pleasure from the smallest things in life, like drinking coffee, reading *The New York Times*, and eating bacon cheeseburgers. After her husband died when my father was young, she decided not to remarry, and lived by herself in the same one-bedroom apartment in Greenwich Village for over fifty years.

When she was in her eighties, Gran was hit by a taxicab while crossing in a crosswalk near Union Square. But the accident didn't stop her—she worked full-time until the age of eighty-four, as a bookkeeper for an advertising firm in Manhattan. She enjoyed walking to work in the morning, and took pride in managing the firm's money, learning how to use a computer and QuickBooks, and being the oldest woman in the office.

When I lived in New York after college, I used to go to her apartment every Friday. She would sit on her red reading chair with white polka dots and tell me that the most meaningful moments in her life were spending time with me and my sister when we were kids. We played a game called "Restaurant," in which Gran would lie in bed and read the paper while my sister and I would take her order and then pretend to cook the food in the kitchen. "You have no idea how much joy you kids brought me," Gran told me. "And to think, I didn't even have to stand up."

I often imagine Gran sitting in her apartment on her red reading chair, one of the last times we were together, saying, "I'm very happy just sitting here with you, Adam. That's all I ever needed." She made me feel like no matter what the world throws at me (even old age and death), I still have something to smile about. Whenever I stress about the future (which is to say, pretty much every day), I remember Gran and the other people I'm grateful for in my life.

Breakthrough Exercise: Express Gratitude

Make a list of five people you're grateful for—they could be family, friends, partners, children, or colleagues. Write a few sentences about why you're grateful for each person. The next time you see them, let them know how much they mean to you. If they live far away, send them a postcard or letter expressing your gratitude.

FOMO → STOP COMPARING YOURSELF TO OTHERS

Social media has made it all but impossible to avoid comparing yourself to others. We see only the coolest parts of our friends' lives, like when they get a new job, win an award, fall in love, or travel somewhere beautiful on Instagram. We think, *Wow, I really need to get my life together.*

Remember my college buddy—the successful lawyer who was getting engaged at Machu Picchu? When I started writing this book, I reached out and asked him how he had figured out everything so easily: job, money, and even marriage.

You know what he told me? That after three years of law school and landing a job at a top firm with a six-figure salary, he was *miserable* in his job as a corporate lawyer, and he was planning on going back to grad school at the age of thirty to become a high school social studies teacher.

What's the lesson here? All of us are figuring it out, even our friends whose Facebook grass looks *really* green. All of us are on different paths, with no right or wrong answer. Comparing yourself to others is a waste of time.

I don't do much one-on-one coaching, because given my skills, I think I can provide more value writing, speaking, and leading career workshops, but when someone approaches me about hiring me as their career coach, I ask them why they want to work with me. If they say anything close to "your life is awesome, I want your life," I don't respond to their e-mail. Don't get me wrong, I love my life—my nickname is Smiley. But it's *my* life. It's not intended to be someone else's.

Trust me, my life isn't for you. I have five roommates. My kitchen has a mouse problem. My sink is constantly full of dishes. There are ants *everywhere*. I bring tea bags with me wherever I go to save the $3 (that adds up to like $90 a month!). I can't for the life of me find a moisturizing cream that works on my hands. I can't drink coffee or alcohol anymore since I have really bad acid reflux. I love to do yoga, but I fart a lot when I do it, so I can't go to class more than once a week—don't get me started about farting during singles yoga. My back is already starting to hurt—and I'm only thirty-two!

These are the kinds of things I spend my time thinking about—it's just not Instagram-worthy material. I can't post a picture of me wallowing in back pain with the caption: "Love my life! #lifeisamazing. Sign up for my 3-step plan to fulfillment now—it's only $495—ahhhhh, my back!"

I refuse to sell some notion that my life is ideal or perfect—that would be inauthentic. All of us (myself included) are sharing our highlight reels on social media, but social media makes life seem rosier than it actually is.

When I talk to people who are considered "successful," they are worried about what they could be doing better. The dude with five thousand Twitter followers wants to be like the dude with one hundred thousand followers. The woman making six figures at Google wants to quit her job and be a freelance writer. The broke freelance writer wants to get a steady job at Google. Success is relative. I'm not advocating that you not learn from others. All of us can improve our work and learn from the best. But it's far more useful to try to live in alignment with who you are than to try to be like someone else.

The journey is personal. I don't know much, but I do know that you won't find the secret to overcoming your quarter-life crisis on Facebook or Instagram; you'll just waste time and start to feel sorry for yourself. Instead, move beyond worrying what other people are doing, and start figuring out what *you* want. What is calling *you*? What mission are *you* drawn to? What goal is worthy of *your* time? Finding meaning is about looking within and listening to the voice inside.

Breakthrough Exercise: Social Media Sabbatical

In order to stop worrying about what *other* people think and start figuring out what *you* want, take a one-week social media sabbatical, beginning on Monday. Don't check your Facebook, Twitter, Instagram, or Snapchat until the following Monday. Trust me: you can do it and it's not impossible. I've done it for two months and survived. In fact, the only reason you're reading this book is because I took time off Facebook to write. If you have to use social media for work, avoid your personal accounts. During your sabbatical, try experimenting daily with a creative activity that you love to do, like writing in your journal, photography, or drawing.

The first part of any quarter-life breakthrough is when a light goes on, alerting you that something in your life isn't working. I'll never forget the moment when my light went on.

In February 2012, I went to a five-day leadership training program called StartingBloc that focuses on social innovation for purpose-driven professionals. At the program in Southern California, I met numerous young people who were in the same situation I was: unfulfilled at work, unwilling to settle for mediocrity, interested in making an impact, and trying to figure out what to do next.

One of those people was Evan Walden. Evan was four years younger than me and had graduated from the University of Vermont in 2009 with a business degree. Interested in joining a start-up but pressured by the fear of postgraduate unemployment during a recession, he decided to take the best job he could find at the largest company that was offering the biggest paycheck. For two years, he sold pesticides for Dow Chemical, covering a $3.5 million territory and overseeing eighty distributor sales representatives.

Despite the recession, Evan went up 30 percent on his sales quotas and received a raise. He was good at selling chemicals, except there was one small problem: he wasn't *interested* in selling chemicals.

Evan says, "When I started at Dow, I experienced a few major things that I found deeply meaningful: living in California for the first time, being able to afford my own place, learning new skills, and being intentionally mentored by someone I admired. But I soon realized I wasn't building networks in the areas that I was most passionate about. The sales skills I was learning were invaluable, but the content of the job was hard for me to relate to. I felt out of place. I was missing a connection to the actual content of my work. Some people say that achieving the mastery of a skill breeds passion, and I think that's true, but when you become good at something, there's a desire to use that talent to affect a system that's bigger than yourself."

Evan's light went on in the summer of 2011, when he visited the Unreasonable Institute, a start-up accelerator program for impact-driven companies in Boulder, Colorado. There, his best friend from college, Nathaniel, was launching ReWork, a company to help people find fulfilling work with social enterprises and nonprofits. When Evan felt himself light up around people who were working with purpose, he knew he was done selling chemicals.

"The day after I returned to California, I looked at myself in the mirror," Evan explains. "I tried to stare as deeply into my own eyes as I possibly could. A familiar feeling of fear washed over me. I felt guilty for wanting to walk away from my commitment. I was uncertain of how I'd pay the bills. But this decision was too important to be made out of fear. I was making this decision out of love. I walked over to the cabinet, took a shot of whiskey, and called my boss. I quit my job and never looked back." Evan moved to Boulder, joining Nathaniel as a cofounder of ReWork.

One evening during StartingBloc, Evan and I were sitting at the rooftop bar of the Shangri-La Hotel, high above Santa Monica's palm trees. We sipped beers and watched the sun set over the Pacific Ocean. After I explained to him my dilemma of feeling stuck in a job that everyone else but me seemed to admire, he asked me one question: "Smiley, are you maximizing your potential?"

"No," I answered without hesitating. "I'm not fully engaged with my work; I'm not present. I want to be somewhere else."

"Why would you be doing anything less than maximizing your potential in life?" Evan asked me. The question hit me like a brick in the head. And at that moment, as the final waves of the day crested and broke under a purple-orange sky, I took a swig of beer and hoisted my hands into the air like I had won an Olympic gold medal. I knew I had to quit my job, and more important, I knew that I *was going to quit my job.*

To be clear: I still had no idea what I was going to do next (this was still more than six months before I moved from DC to San Francisco). But I knew then that my breakthrough had begun. That was the first time, after feeling stuck for at least a year, that I felt empowered to make a change. Not once after that moment did I ever feel my Morning Edition, that brutal pain shooting up and down my spine.

The most significant moment of a breakthrough is beginning to listen to the voice within.

BREAKTHROUGH TAKEAWAYS

- If you want to turn your quarter-life crisis into a breakthrough and move beyond feeling stuck, hopeless, and overcome with FOMO, take tangible steps to explore what you're interested in.
- Express gratitude for the people in your life and the opportunities you have. Resist what can be so tempting—to compare yourself to others—and listen to the voice within, the one that's telling you to make a change.

The first part of any quarter-life breakthrough is when a light goes on, alerting you that something in your life isn't working. Pay attention when this light goes on, even if you're not sure what's next.

CHAPTER 3

Embrace Fear

"You can choose courage or you can choose comfort.
You cannot have both."
—BRENÉ BROWN

Two weeks after StartingBloc, when I had that invincible feeling that I could do anything, Evan called me to check in while I was at work in Washington, DC. "Did you have 'the talk' with your boss yet?" he asked me.

"No," I admitted.

"Why not?" he pressed.

"I don't know, I'll do it soon. This isn't a good month."

"*Smiley* . . . ," he said skeptically. "What do you mean this isn't a good month?"

"Well, I'm scared," I said. "My boss told me I'm doing a great job and that I might get a raise soon, and my roommate told me to wait for my matching 401(k) plan to kick in next year, and then I could have noncompetitive eligibility, a huge asset for federal employees."

"Whoa, wait a second," Evan fired back at me. "You told me you didn't want to stay in DC, or work for the government anymore—you told me you were ready to leap now."

"I *am* ready to leap now," I said.

"So . . . what the hell are you waiting for?" asked Evan.

The truth was that I wasn't scared about leaving my job—I was terrified. Even though I knew I was ready to quit, the fear of leaping into a new career path at the age of twenty-eight nearly crippled me. Even though I had determined that the most important thing to me was finding fulfilling work, I *still* felt pressured to play it safe.

Fear is a powerful force that can derail people's hopes and dreams. The journey requires *courage*—no one said it was going to be easy. If fear had gotten the best of us, you wouldn't be reading this book right now, Ryan would still be eating Hot Pockets every night for dinner, and Evan would still be selling chemicals somewhere in southern California.

During my quarter-life breakthrough, there were three fears I learned to embrace to help guide me to my next lily pad:

1. Fear of the unknown
2. Fear of what others will think
3. Fear of too many options

This chapter will teach you how not to run from these fears, but to use them as a source of positive energy and motivation.

FEAR IS A SIGN

One of my mentors is twenty-five-year-old Ted Gonder. You may think it's odd for someone who is thirty-two to have a mentor who is seven years younger, but that's because you haven't met Ted, an all-around badass. When Ted was in high school, he was interested in starting a small climate change awareness club. Someone told him he should turn the club into a national movement and call Bill Clinton and Al Gore to get their support. Ted thought the guy was nuts, but he made the call anyway. On the first couple of calls, he got nothing but an answering machine. After a couple of tries, he eventually received a callback from Al Gore's COO, asking him to join the Climate Reality Project as the student advisor and to help launch a network of climate change awareness clubs in public schools across the country. Ted has been embracing fear ever since those first phone calls.

In 2009, in the wake of the country's economic collapse, Ted cofounded Moneythink, a Chicago-based nonprofit that teaches financial skills and entrepreneurial thinking to urban high school students. As someone who grew up with a lot of privilege, he became inspired to teach young people with less access how to manage their money, avoid debt, and start businesses. He's currently Moneythink's CEO and recently advised (yes, advised!) the Department of Homeland Security on ways to increase opportunities for immigrant entrepreneurs to come to the United States to work.

Ted gives an inspiring talk to young entrepreneurs called "Smashing Fear," which I've seen three times. During the talk, he shows YouTube videos of the fearless honey badger sticking his head into a swarming beehive to extract the larvae. He also talks about his personal credo, one all of us can aspire to: Fear is a tool, fear is fuel, fear is to be partnered with, we can listen to our fears to point us in the direction we need to walk. Ted says, "If we think of fear as an accomplice rather than an enemy, then we can be free to lean into it, and pursue our dreams, ideas, and projects freely."

In order to demonstrate the principle that anyone with courage can become an official fear smasher, Ted hands out limes to everyone in the audience at the end of the talk. He asks everyone to bite into a whole lime to suck all the juice out (don't eat the peel!). It's hard to replicate this activity, but there's an energy in the room when everyone is chomping into limes and hurling the skins to the ground.

Rather than a sign of encouragement or motivation, fear all too often becomes a red light that puts the brakes on the very ideas, goals, and journeys that are right for us. Try shifting your perspective to view fear as a green light, an indicator that you're moving in the right direction.

Breakthrough Exercise: Fear Is a Sign

Write down one thing you're scared of doing (like quitting your job, experimenting with a new career path, launching a project, or moving to a new city). Ask yourself: Why are you scared of doing this? Why does it frighten you? Is it scary because it's what you know you need to do?

LISTEN TO YOUR VOICE, NOT THE OTHER VOICES

Fear always strikes at the most untimely moments. I knew I was ready to leave my job at the Peace Corps, and as soon as I was getting excited about my plan to become a freelance writer, my parents, my boss, my coworkers, and even my close friends started telling me what a great job I had.

I had all these voices in my head telling me things like: play it safe, think about your 401(k) plan, you're so good at your job, quitting is going to affect your résumé, you have a great job—think about all the people who have master's degrees who would kill for your job.

These voices are incredibly powerful, and they can stifle a breakthrough. To ensure that this doesn't happen, it's important to differentiate between which of these fears are actually *yours* and which of them are merely voices in your head from all the conversations you have every day with *other people*.

When I did this exercise, I realized that one of the fears preventing me from leaving my job was a recurring voice in my head that wasn't my own; rather, it was the voice of several *coworkers* telling me I had a great job.

I asked myself: why would my coworkers ever tell me to leave my job if they liked working with me so much? I decided to *listen to the voice within*, take away all the advice everyone else had given me, and make the decision that was right for me. I also decided to *stop comparing myself to others* and remember that it doesn't matter what other people think. All that matters is that I know I'm ready to explore other interests.

An important caveat: it's not that your colleagues, parents, boss, and friends don't love you or that their advice is necessarily bad advice. They do love you, and their advice might be perfectly sound. But people usually give advice that reflects their own experiences. Your coworker, who has stayed in the same job for ten years, is probably not going to tell you to quit your job after two years. Someone like me, who recently quit my job to pursue my dream, is probably not going to tell you to stay in the same job for ten years if you're unhappy.

Your parents, who love you more than the world and want what's *safe* for you, might not know what's *right* for you. I have a friend who is in his fourth year of medical school, and deciding what he specializes in for residency. The decision will impact the next four years, as well as his career path for many years to come. He's interested in specializing in family medicine, but worried because his parents would be happier if he pursued a more prestigious field like surgery. This exemplifies how impossible it is to please our parents—as if going to med school and becoming a doctor isn't enough, our parents care about the *type of doctor* we're going to become.

Many young people I meet end up pursuing paths out of parental pressure, rather than personal alignment. This often leads to confusion and resentment, and sometimes unhappiness. Trying to please your parents with your life choices, in my opinion, is futile. Most parents are impossible to please, and what they think is right for you is based on their own personal experiences, or something they heard once on NPR, not what's actually right for you.

A parent's job is to make sure their child survives. It's your job to figure out what you actually want; it's your job to *thrive*. At the end of the day, the journey is personal: you're the only one who knows what's right for you. There's a *Seinfeld* episode in which George Costanza claims that he invented the "it's not you, it's me" routine. Get in the habit of saying, *It's not you, it's me.*

Even people you look up to, even people who work in a career field you're interested in, can give advice that's not right for you. Before I left my job at the Peace Corps, I had coffee with one of my favorite journalists, an award-winning staff writer for *The New Yorker*. I told her I was thinking of leaving my job to move to San Francisco and start writing about subjects I was really interested in, and you know what she told me? "Don't quit your day job." Even though I completely respect her and her work, I chose to ignore her advice and listen to the voice within, remembering, *It's not you, it's me.*

DOUBT YOUR DOUBT

During a recent career coaching session, my client "Laura" told me she was feeling drained in her job as an account manager for a marketing consulting firm. The firm was based three thousand miles away, in New York City, and Laura worked remotely from San Francisco. I asked her what wasn't working for her, and she said she was tired of working remotely on her own, and that she wished she had a more collaborative team. She also expressed that her own health had suffered as a result of her job, so she was looking to get into the health and wellness space and help others maintain a healthier diet and regular exercise regimen.

Laura had reached out to me because she felt lost and stuck in her career. I told her it didn't sound like she was lost at all; she seemed to know exactly what she was looking for. When I pressed Laura, it was clear that she wasn't stuck, but rather overcome with doubt, the voice in her head keeping her from making the leap to a new lily pad. I asked Laura to write down her doubts about making the transition to a job in health and wellness. Here's what she wrote:

I'm not qualified.
The market is saturated.
There's no money in health and wellness.
I'll have to work long hours to prove myself since I'm new to the field.
I might need a degree or license to work in health. How will I pay
    for a new license?
What happens in two years if it doesn't work out and I'm unhappy?

Laura wasn't alone in doubting herself. I know I certainly had my doubts when I left my job at the Peace Corps. Fear of the unknown often kept me up all night. Three years later, I still have doubts about my path. I wonder, How can I be thirty-two and still have five roommates? How will I make enough money as a writer to have a family one day? The doubt never goes away, but I've learned that we can turn our doubts into research, into positive energy that takes us closer to our next lily pad.

Below each of her doubts, Laura and I wrote the answer to the question: Is this a fear inside my head, or an actual fact I've researched? Here's what we learned:

I'm not qualified.
Fact or fear? FEAR. I don't know if I'm not qualified yet since I have no idea what position I'm actually applying for. I may actually be qualified for some roles.

The market is saturated.
Fact or fear? FEAR. I don't know if the market is saturated since I haven't actually started applying for new jobs.

There's no money in health and wellness.
Fact or fear? FEAR. Fitbit has received over $50 million in investment capital and gone public, so there's at least some money in health and wellness.

I'll have to work long hours to prove myself since I'm new to the field.
Fact or fear? FACT. But I work long hours in my current job, and everyone starting a new job has to prove herself.

I might need a degree or license to work in health. How will I pay for a new license?
Fact or fear? FACT (maybe). I may need a license, but it's possible some companies might provide training or even pay for me to get licensed.

What happens in two years if it doesn't work out and I'm unhappy?
Fact or fear? FEAR. Only the genie in *Aladdin* knows what will
happen in two years. Maybe I'll be happy. If I'm unhappy, I can make
another change.

Identifying her doubts helped Laura to go from being scared of the
voices in her head to taking action. She realized she couldn't make an in-
formed decision about whether to change jobs until she did more research
about the health and wellness space and discovered what she was interested in.

After our session, Laura met with a professional wellness coach to ask
questions and learn more about her practice, and came up with a list of
organizations she wanted to learn more about. Laura's research helped her
realize that she was interested in utilizing her marketing and communications skills for a company in the health and wellness space, and that she
didn't need an advanced degree or a license to get to her next lily pad. By
getting her doubts out of her head and written down on paper, she was able
to take tangible steps toward her breakthrough.

Breakthrough Exercise: Fact or Fear?

Write down any doubts you're having about your breakthrough.

Below each, clarify whether the doubt is a FACT (something you've
actually researched) or a FEAR (a fictional story that is in your head).

FEAR OF TOO MANY OPTIONS WILL KEEP YOU STUCK

Do you have trouble focusing or making decisions? Me too. I think every
person born after 1980 has trouble focusing and making decisions. I can go
from writing a sentence of this book, to checking my e-mail, to checking

Facebook, to texting my friend to see if she wants to meet up later for a drink, to eating some almonds, to reading the BuzzFeed article my friend just posted, to checking the home page of *The New York Times*, all within forty-five seconds.

The problem is that sometimes we act like this when it comes to major life decisions, and it paralyzes us. When I first was thinking about my breakthrough, I was all over the place. I considered becoming an English teacher, a freelance writer, and working at a nonprofit that produces documentaries.

I was too afraid to make the wrong decision, so I made no decision at all. Fear of too many options kept me stuck. It's a fact of life that there are always two or more options and you could always be somewhere else. Remember: the grass is always greener. A good way to begin figuring out which option is the right fit for you is to take concrete steps toward determining which fits you best. Take a class in something you're interested in learning more about, read industry books and blogs, and talk to people working in areas you care about.

In the upcoming chapters, we'll discuss how you can avoid being stuck by trying many opportunities that interest you in the form of apprenticeships, internships, crowdfunding campaigns, and short-term side projects. This way, you can evaluate whether something is a fit in a shorter period of time. We'll also discuss how to determine whether an opportunity is financially viable for you.

Every time you leap to another lily pad, you get a little bit closer to what you're looking for. Learning what's not the right fit is just as valuable as learning what is. I never would have done StartingBloc, moved to San Francisco, worked for the Bold Academy and Hive, started a blog, gotten published, or written this book if it hadn't been for my job at the Peace Corps—which might make it the most meaningful job I've ever had, precisely because it pushed me closer to realizing who I am and what I *actually* wanted to do.

BREAKTHROUGH TAKEAWAYS

- Fear is a powerful force that can derail a breakthrough. Common fears include *fear of the unknown, fear of what others will think,* and *fear of too many options.* Fear is universal, and trying to avoid it is futile. To get where you need to go, embrace fear to guide your journey instead of fighting it. Use fear as an indicator that you're on the right path.
- Be aware of whether your doubts about your breakthrough are coming from another source, like your parents, boss, coworkers, friends, or society.

Remember to clarify whether your doubts are actually based on research you've done or are merely fears in your head.

PART TWO

Find Meaningful Work

PART TWO

CHAPTER 4

Define Meaningful Work

"Our job in this lifetime is not to shape ourselves into some ideal we imagine we ought to be, but to find out who we already are and become it."
—STEVEN PRESSFIELD, *The War of Art*

EVAN ASKED ME a question on that rooftop in Santa Monica that has stayed with me ever since: "Why would you be doing anything less than maximizing your full potential in life?"

People maximize their potential when they work toward something greater than themselves and when they align their work with their purpose. Another way to think of your **purpose** is *what you want to do for the world.* When people reach their full potential, they change the world because they know *why* they're doing what they're doing. In my case, my current purpose is to help others reach their full potential through writing, public speaking, and facilitating transformative experiences like the Hive Global Leaders Program.

Recall our definition of meaningful work from the introduction: **Meaningful work provides personal meaning, reflecting who you are and what your interests are; allows you to share your gifts to help others; provides a community of believers that will support your dreams; and is financially viable given your desired lifestyle**.

A lot of books about finding meaningful work ask you to determine your calling in life. Those books scare the hell out of me. In this chapter we're simply going to ask the right questions to figure out *what your purpose is now*, so you can figure out which lily pad to leap to next.

Let's accept the idea that very few people have only one purpose, one truth, or one calling. Our purpose actually changes throughout our lives as we try different jobs, travel to new places, meet new people, and grow older. Over the last thirty years, I've had numerous different "callings," from being Big Bird to being a sportswriter to making movies—and I'm currently doing none of those things.

We each have to define meaning for ourselves and accept that our definition might change over time. For example, Ryan was satisfied selling e-mail marketing software for many years, until the time came when he wanted to spend his days doing something more meaningful.

In this chapter, we'll break down our definition of meaningful work into six parts, and ask a few basic questions that will lead to complex answers. Your responses will get you closer to realizing how you can maximize your potential by aligning your work with your purpose.

DEFINING MEANINGFUL WORK

Part 1: Meaningful Work Reflects Who You Are

While I was at StartingBloc, it was daunting to realize that I was twenty-eight years old and *still* hadn't figured out who I was. Sure, on paper, I had *everything* figured out: I had a job, a nice apartment, great benefits, and girls (occasionally) would go out with me. But the truth was that I hadn't yet discovered *why I was here.*

To try to figure out my purpose during my breakthrough, I read *What Color is Your Parachute?* (for the second time), took a Myers-Briggs personality test and completed StrengthsFinder, did lots of yoga, and contemplated going on a pilgrimage to a temple somewhere in Asia, but decided that buying a $1,500 plane ticket would be unwise, given the fact that I was going to quit my job in a few months.

While all of these tools can be helpful, it turns out that the most useful thing I did cost no money at all. I broke out my Moleskine journal and wrote down the answers to a series of self-discovery questions, which I've included in the upcoming exercises. If these questions seem rudimentary, that's because they are. However, many people go much of their adult lives without ever asking themselves these questions, which might explain why 70 percent of the US population spend their days disengaged at work.

"What's the first thing people notice about you?" is one of the questions that you are encouraged to answer when setting up your online dating profile on OkCupid. I prefer the related but more relevant question: *What do you love about yourself?*

When I first asked myself this question, I answered as if I were in a job interview. I assumed my greatest asset was my hard work ethic and my ability to multitask. After some reflection, I realized that what I love about myself actually has nothing to do with the workplace whatsoever. What I love about myself is my ability to laugh and smile despite all the trouble in the world and stress in my life. I think I inherited this attitude of "it could always be worse" from my grandparents, who lost everything in the Depression and faced problems a lot more serious than having Facebook-induced FOMO.

When I say that I smile a lot, it might be an understatement. I got the nickname "Smiley" my second week of high school. I wanted to play a sport. I wasn't good enough to make the soccer team. Football was out of the question since I was about five feet tall and 110 pounds. I wasn't coordinated enough to do crew. The only other option was cross-country. So I went to practice. I didn't even know what cross-country was, and I looked at the coach like he was nuts when he told us to go run five miles along the Charles River.

"Wait, we just go running?" I asked.

"Yes, kid, we run, that's what we do, what did you think this was?" he said.

"I actually have no idea," I replied. "It sounded fun."

My coach, an all-American runner in high school, was also from Cambridge. One chilly day, we were running a hill workout, which involved running up and down a huge hill, over and over again. About fourteen hills in, exhausted, I was nearing the top of the hill, digging in and struggling with a big grin on my face. "What the hell-aah-ya-doin' smilin', kid?!" my coach screamed at me in his thick Boston accent. "Yaaah not supposed to be smilin', yaaah supposed to be pukin', staaaup smilin', staaaht pukin', staaaht pukin', kid!"

From then on, the team called me Smiley. This is a core piece of my personality that needs to be present in my day-to-day life. I don't want to feel like I need to put on an "act" at the office, or try to be someone I'm not. I want to be able to show up every day as myself, unwavering smile and all.

Breakthrough Exercise: Where Your Heart Resides

Try answering as many of these questions as you can, writing without stopping as you move through each question. Don't judge the answer, just write what comes to mind. If you prefer to just reflect on them, that's okay, too. Do what works for you.

What do you love about yourself?
How are you different from your friends?
What makes you, you?
What makes you weird? (Being weird is a good thing.)
Who do you want to show up as every day?
What memories do you have of when you were a kid?
What is your most sacred memory of spending time with
a grandparent? Parent? Sibling?
What do you really like to do?
What do you absolutely hate doing?
When was the last time you were really happy?
When was the last time you cried?

Part 2: Meaningful Work Reflects Your Interests

We have to figure out for ourselves what we care most about, and these interests often evolve. Ryan grew up a computer geek, but a trip to Uganda changed his interests. The reason I wanted to work at the Peace Corps was because the job deeply aligned with issues I cared about. I believed in the Peace Corps' mission to promote world peace and friendship, and I believed in the work eight thousand Peace Corps volunteers were doing in remote communities all over the world.

Sometimes we don't have to look too far to find the personal experience that shapes our interests, and how to incorporate our interests into our work. Tom D'Eri, twenty-six, had been interested in social innovation and sustainable business since early on in college at Bentley University. Upon graduation, he considered positions in corporate social responsibility, but the corporate world didn't move him. Instead, he went back to an idea he had in college that was inspired by his brother Andrew, who has autism.

Although his brother is a vibrant young man, Tom saw that his brother's disability put him at a clear disadvantage when it came to securing meaningful employment. Tom returned home to South Florida to run Rising Tide Car Wash alongside his father. The family business employs and empowers people with autism, and provides people of all ability levels an opportunity to build a career and an independent life.

Tom explained to me that his company provides meaning to his employees because, for the first time in many of their lives, they have an opportunity to provide something valuable to others. They also get to be part of a community that celebrates what makes them unique. "As novel as a job at a car wash may be to the average person," Tom explains, "we're seeing tremendous improvement in our employees' self-esteem and social skills." Rising Tide also provides meaning to its customers because they can vote with their dollars, making the business case for employing individuals with disabilities.

We often think of interests as academic subjects like art, history, or science. But interests are really anything that energizes you. For Tom, that meant his own family and the challenges facing people with disabilities that he had seen firsthand. By picking a cause near to his heart, Tom embarked on a journey to build a business that provides personal meaning to him, as well as meaning to his employees and customers.

It turns out that Tom wasn't the only one passionate about empowering people with autism. Tom was accepted to the Unreasonable Institute, a five-week fellowship for social entrepreneurs that introduced him to world-class mentors and investors, and a Rising Tide Car Wash video has now been viewed thirty million times and shared nine hundred thousand times on Facebook and YouTube.

Some entrepreneurs might be satisfied with viral fame and a few press clips. Not Tom. Tom's purpose goes far beyond his personal brand and Rising Tide Car Wash; Tom's purpose is to help *other* businesses employ people with autism. To this end, Rising Tide Car Wash has piloted an operations and management leadership program for impact-driven millennials who want to start their own businesses or work for businesses that will employ people with disabilities. With this effort, Tom and his family are passing the torch, helping spread the knowledge of what they've learned to more and more people.

I was curious what advice Tom had for other young people looking for mission-driven work. "When I was in school, I held the mentality that most high-achieving students do, that I should be given an opportunity to do awesome strategy and consulting work right out of school because I'm really smart and people should listen to what I have to say," Tom said. "Frankly, I'm embarrassed that I held that view. In all honesty, just because you graduate summa cum laude doesn't mean you know jack. In my mind, the best way to build a career with meaning and gain the respect of your peers, is from the boots up. This means don't look down on any role, listen to the people you're working with, ask them questions about why they are where they are, and work your ass off to grow the skill sets you're passionate about by seeking out difficult situations, great mentors, and supplementing your work experience by reading as much as you possibly can."

Tom makes it clear that humility is an important part of meaningful work. While Tom found work that aligned with his personal interests, his goal wasn't merely personal fulfillment. It was service to his brother, service to people with disabilities, and service to other young people seeking to become leaders. When you launch a career driven by purpose, everyone wins.

Part 3: Meaningful Work Allows You to Share Your Gifts

A lot of inspirational blogs simply tell you to "follow your passion!" My response is, "If I knew what my one passion was, I wouldn't be reading your blog." From my experience, it's far easier to find meaningful work if you use your unique gifts (your strengths and skills) as your calling card alongside your interests, rather than your passion (or in my case, my eleven passions).

For example, I'm deeply passionate about making others laugh. I smile so often that whenever I'm at a bar, bulky dudes with tattoos and baseball caps look at me like they're about to pound my face into the *Big Buck Hunter* arcade machine. I love Larry David and Dave Chappelle, but this doesn't mean I want to work as a stand-up comedian.

Instead, I want work that allows me to share my gifts with the world:

writing, public speaking, spreading positive energy, interacting with people, and creating transformative experiences that help purpose-driven leaders.

Many people who find their work fulfilling have achieved some degree of expertise in their work. It feels great to be good at something. Skills often get people hired, and they usually determine what you'll be doing for eight to ten hours a day.

Skills can also provide leverage and allow you to take your career in multiple directions, which is ever more important in an unstable job market. I've been able to utilize my writing and communications skills to pursue a range of opportunities in film, government, publishing, and leadership development programs.

If you want to read more about why skills matter, check out Cal Newport's excellent book *So Good They Can't Ignore You: Why Skills Trump Passion in the Quest for Work You Love*, or Daniel H. Pink's *Drive: The Surprising Truth about What Motivates Us*. Before we move on, I want to share a few important points about skills.

IF YOU'RE GOOD AT SOMETHING YOU DON'T LIKE DOING, FIND SOMETHING ELSE TO BE GOOD AT

When I worked at the Peace Corps, I spent the majority of my days doing administrative tasks: scheduling meetings and conference calls, compiling to-do lists, drafting memos, and planning events, to name a few. I happen to be very good at detail-oriented administrative work—years of neuroses have made me a meticulous planner. Sometimes I even write to-do lists of things I've *already done*, because it makes me feel good to cross them off. My boss and my teammates loved working with me because I used to keep us all on task and goal-oriented.

The only problem was that I didn't actually *like* doing detail-oriented administrative work. I hated scheduling meetings, making agendas, and trying to get memos approved in a bureaucracy. I wanted to do more writing and creative projects. It's nice to know that I have a practical skill if I ever need a job in the future doing project management, administrative work, or event planning, but it's also important to recognize when something you're good at is not the right fit. In the end, it wasn't that I didn't enjoy working at the Peace Corps—an incredible organization full of brilliant colleagues and that aligned with my interests—it's that I didn't enjoy what I was doing every day from nine to five (or more like eight to eight).

Being good at something can get you a great job. However, having a skill you're good at but that you hate doing may keep you from finding meaningful work. In the next exercise, you'll differentiate between things you're good at that make you miserable and things you're good at that you love.

If You Need to Develop a New Skill, Start Learning Now

A lot of people only pursue things they're naturally good at, which is fine if you want to be a playwright and you've been writing plays since the second grade. But it was problematic for someone like me, who decided he wanted to start writing after not taking a single English class in college and spending his first seven years after graduation working in film and politics. If you want to pursue something you don't know much about or something you're not very good at, *admit what you don't know and take steps immediately toward learning more and improving that skill.*

At the age of twenty-eight, when I decided that I wanted to pursue writing, I hadn't published anything besides articles for my high school and college newspapers. While still working at the Peace Corps, I started having coffee with every single writer I knew to ask how they got started and how they practiced writing. I read books on writing like Anne Lamott's *Bird by Bird*, Julia Cameron's *The Artist's Way*, and Steven Pressfield's *The War of Art*. Most important, I followed my freelance-writer friend Ryan's advice and took a small step: I created a blog and started writing regularly.

Millennials are known for being job-hoppers, but some research shows that millennial job-hopping is a myth—young workers are actually staying in their jobs longer than previous generations. Still, if the average millennial is staying in their job for three years, this means that some of us will have as many as fifteen to twenty jobs during our career, which can be costly for organizations. Companies spend millions of dollars a year trying to hire the right people—one study by PricewaterhouseCoopers found that unanticipated turnover can cost companies 20 to 200 percent of the employee's original salary.

If you think you're a restless millennial who can't stay in one job, meet Yoni Binstock. Over the past three years, Yoni has been employed by six different companies. Six jobs in three years is a lot. Don't worry, I'm not advocating you quit your job every six months—I want to share the cure to Yoni's job frustration with you. Yoni wasn't doing anything wrong as he explored different possibilities—he was interested in working with smart people and making a difference, so he worked at innovative, mission-driven companies like Ashoka, DailyFeats, Mosaic, SolarCity, and Change.org, holding entry-level roles in a variety of areas including business development, marketing, strategic partnerships, and sales.

In his best-selling book *Drive*, Daniel H. Pink uses decades of scientific research to identify three core elements that motivate our work. The first motivation is **autonomy**: having control over your work, choosing what projects you work on, and having freedom to determine how you work. The second is **mastery**: developing a skill and becoming really good at something. When was the last time you met a symphony conductor, or the chef at a Michelin-starred restaurant, who hated their job? Being an expert in what you do is fulfilling. The third is **purpose**: making a difference with your work, and contributing to something larger than yourself.

Yoni soon realized that working for impact-driven companies was important to him, but not as important as *how he was spending his time and what he was learning* at those companies. Interested in becoming a software engineer, he decided to take an immersive twelve-week web development program at General Assembly, which cost $11,500. He chose a coding class for a few reasons. First, his wife had just graduated from the program, and got a job at a Fortune 500 company two weeks after graduating. Second, he wanted to learn a skill set that would last the next few decades of outsourcing and automation. Last, he had spent a lot of money hiring developers on personal projects, and wanted the ability to code his own apps and build awesome things every day.

Mastery Leads to Meaning

For his next lily pad, Yoni's primary motivation was *mastery*: he focused on becoming a really good coder. After completing the immersive front-end development course at General Assembly, he got a three-month contract at Hot Schedules, and then a full-time job as a software engineer at Mobolet, a food truck review web and mobile application. The career coaches at General Assembly helped him to refine his résumé and interview skills, and even made personal introductions to prospective companies.

"At Mobolet, I'm coding nearly all day long," said Yoni. "Every day, I'm faced with a problem I've never seen before and have no idea how to solve. Using whiteboards, Google, Stack Overflow, and with the help of my colleagues, I piece together the problem and slowly manage to find a solution. But that's what makes it so meaningful, the difficulty of the challenges and overcoming them every day."

I asked Yoni whether taking the class was worth it. "Not only was it worth it, it was probably the best financial decision my wife and I will make in our lives," Yoni said. "We've doubled our salaries, and the market demand for our skills is only growing. The goals we have for our lives together are now made possible with our new skill set."

Yoni found a new motivation for his work through mastering a new skill. His new job at Mobolet is full-time remote, which allows him the flexibility and the freedom to work from home, or anywhere in the world he wants. Yoni and his wife, Maia, are planning to spend next year traveling and working remotely all around Southeast Asia.

Knowing Yoni, if I were a betting man I'd wager that he doesn't stay at this job forever. But I'm guessing that because he is learning so much on the job, and developing expertise in a skill that matters to him, he'll stay longer than six months. When he does leave, he'll do so with a lot more mastery, autonomy, and purpose than when he started.

It's intimidating to begin learning a new skill like Yoni did with programming or I did with writing. Be okay with being a beginner. Everyone has to start somewhere.

Breakthrough Exercise: Discovering Your Gifts

Make a list of *everything* you're good at, including things like baking and break dancing, not only résumé skills like Microsoft Excel and grant writing. Think about things you were really good at as a kid, in high school, and during college. These are your unique skills and strengths, your gifts to the world.

Now cross off the things on this list that you don't actually *like* doing. For the remaining items, in what areas do you need to deepen your knowledge? What types of classes do you need to take? What books do you need to read? What experts do you need to talk to?

Pick one thing on that list that you need to deepen your knowledge of or start learning about—and then explore concrete ways to improve that skill.

Part 4: Meaningful Work Allows You to Help Others

Now it's time to bring the pieces of your meaningful work definition together: what holds your personality, your interests, and your gifts in place is *how* you're going to help others. By this I mean, determining *what type of impact* you want to make.

Although there are infinite ways people can make an impact with their work, I find it helpful to ask a few questions: *Do I need to see the results of my work every single day? Do I need to have a face-to-face relationship with the people I'm serving, or can I make an indirect impact behind the scenes?*

Face-to-face impact implies that you're working with the person you're helping on a daily basis, allowing you to see the purpose of your work up close. Think of people on the front lines: a classroom teacher, an aid worker, a community organizer, a coach, or a doctor.

You can also make an indirect impact. You may not see your impact on a daily basis, but you know that over time, your work is contributing toward a cause greater than yourself. There's an element of delayed gratification. Think of the people behind the scenes: a research scientist, a policy analyst, a programmer, or a consultant.

From my experience working at the Peace Corps, I learned that it was not enough for me to be working behind the scenes for administrators, drafting memos and enhancing agency policies in Washington, DC, which impacted over eight thousand volunteers working in seventy-five countries. My experience taught me the valuable lesson that, personally, I would have been a lot more fulfilled working face-to-face with several villagers in rural Botswana than drafting memos in a cubicle in a five-hundred-person office building in the nation's capital. Learning *how* you want to do your work is equally as valuable as learning *what* you want to do in the first place.

Gayle Abrams's journey to figure out how to share her gifts as an educator is a great example of this idea. Gayle, twenty-nine, has been a teacher for the past eight years and once invited me to visit her classroom when I lived in DC.

Geoffrey Canada, founder of the Harlem Children's Zone, once said, "When you see a great teacher, you are seeing a work of art." When I first heard this quote, I immediately thought of Gayle. Gayle has the uncanny ability to light up a classroom, using games and jokes to get her fourth graders excited about learning. Thirty minutes into their geometry lesson, each of her students had demonstrated the difference between parallel, perpendicular, and intersecting lines, and were competing in a game to point out as many examples of each in the classroom—one kid even spotted perpendicular lines on my blue marine-themed socks.

Gayle loves both math and teaching—she once choreographed a dance with her class to Daft Punk's "Around the World," and then performed it with them in the school talent show. But her work nearly drove her to the point of burnout. As Gayle describes, "I was working as a math specialist in an urban elementary school, teaching fourth-grade math . . . I gave every bit of my being to teaching my fourth graders math conceptually, with the goal that they would succeed on the standardized assessment. And they did—with results that my school district had never seen before. The pressure I put on myself was worth it. But the following year the pressure to maintain that level of success caused my eye to twitch for three months straight.

"I came home each night hanging by a thread. I felt like I was failing my students. I couldn't motivate and engage all of them. My identity had become so wrapped up in my work. I knew the only way I could fully gain any sense of clarity was to take a step back."

Feeling drained (understandably so—Gayle treats math class like others treat Zumba), Gayle explored options in math education outside of the classroom. She took a job as a math education consultant for a professional development company called Math Solutions. In her role, she traveled around the Northeast and Midwest, providing on-site professional development and coaching to middle school and high school math teachers whose students were struggling with mathematics.

Instead of merely having an impact on her classroom of twenty-five students, as a coach she changed the way math teachers in schools across the country light up their classrooms. She quickly found that working directly with teachers was just as rewarding as working with students. "Now I get to hear stories of other teachers and learn from their perspectives, so that maybe one day I'll be able to go back into the classroom with a sense of balance and resilience I was missing," says Gayle.

There are a variety of needs within any field or career, and the impact we want to make may be different at twenty-five and at thirty. We need talented teachers in the classroom, talented people to train teachers, and talented people to set the policies and standards to ensure that what kids are actually learning will help them become engaged global citizens.

Gayle's story is one of flexibility and experimentation. By making a small pivot within her career, she found meaningful work. The question for

Gayle was not *Is it more impactful to be a classroom teacher, or a math education coach?* Both of these options are impactful in one way or another—the goal is to determine whether an opportunity allows you to make the type of impact you want to make right now.

A year after working for Math Solutions, a new lily pad appeared for Gayle. She and her husband, Ian, had their first baby boy, Emory. In order to spend as much time with Emory as possible, Gayle chose to work half-time as an instructional coach at a local charter school. "As a teacher I spent most of my time getting to know other people's children—helping them become perseverant, confident, and community-minded individuals," said Gayle. "It was important to me to be able to spend time building a bond with my own child and learning how to be the mom Emory deserves. As he's growing and becoming more interested in the world around him, I'm recognizing that part of being a great mom for me means maintaining my identity as an educator and working to improve instructional experiences for children in my city."

When Emory gets older, Gayle wants to go back to the classroom full-time. I find her story inspiring, because she has been able to keep teaching, alongside the challenges of raising a child. In fact, Gayle has learned that being a mom makes her a better teacher. Personally, I've always wondered whether having kids and pursuing meaningful work are mutually exclusive. To get vulnerable, I'll admit that having kids scares the crap out of me because I think it means I'll immediately have to stop writing, trade in my bicycle for a minivan, and move to the suburbs. I'm not sure why I have that recurring nightmare, but I do.

"You can definitely be a parent, even a great parent, and still make your career a priority," Gayle told me. "I think there is a misconception that we believe being great at something means you alone kick ass at it. We are good parents and good at our jobs because we depend on our community, and we try to be proactive and prioritize what's important. We made a family schedule on Google Calendar to hold ourselves accountable to what we care about most: family dinner, date night, exercising, and spending time with our friends."

Part of the reason Gayle has been able to pursue meaningful work is because she and her husband, Ian, are a true team. They rely on each other (and their community) for support. Ian's stable job as a solar energy installer has helped support Gayle and Emory. As Ian considers starting his own solar business, Gayle will be there to support him as well. You never know when you're going to have to make a change to your work life, and you never know what's going to cause that change. But as long as you're willing to be flexible and adapt like Gayle has done, you'll keep finding the lily pad that works for you.

Breakthrough Exercise: Impact

Reflect on the following questions, either in writing or aloud:

What type of impact do you want to have?
What type of impact have you had in previous jobs?
Do you need to see the results of your work every single day?
Do you need to have a face-to-face relationship with the people you're serving?

Part 5: Meaningful Work Provides a Community of Believers That Will Support Your Dreams

My friend Lauren Weinstein has been a professional coach for four years. She became a coach while working for Accenture, and later completed Georgetown's leadership coaching program. She recently faced a key inflection point in her career, having to decide whether to keep consulting for multiple organizations or to work full-time for one organization. Contrary to the popular belief that setting your own schedule leads to freedom and fulfillment, Lauren's decision was to stop consulting and take one full-time job as a program officer for talent at the Charles and Lynn Schusterman

Family Foundation, which seeks to empower young people to create positive change for themselves, the Jewish community, and the world. She told me her decision drivers were the following:

- Wanting to have a targeted vision and focus, versus feeling scattered working on multiple projects.
- Wanting a clearer distinction between work and personal life. It's very challenging when you run your own business to turn off and relax.
- Wanting to have supportive peers and a mission-aligned team.

Interestingly, Lauren's full-time job provides her more free time than when she ran her own business, because she's now able to turn off when she's not at work. For some people, like Yoni, who's headed off to code in Southeast Asia, autonomy may mean being able to work from anywhere and set your own schedule; for others, it means freedom to choose the type of projects you care about. Working for Schusterman offers Lauren the advantage of having the resources, both financial and creative, to make things happen. She is able to collaborate with experts in the talent development field, and organizations like the Center for Creative Leadership, resources that would be less easily available if she worked on her own. She also has a supportive boss and dynamic team that encourage her to make things happen.

"While working on my own, I was constantly thinking about how much money each deal was," explains Lauren. "I know, it sounds horrible, but as I was trying to build my own business, I was worrying a lot about money and paying the bills. Now I think more about impact, how many people's lives I touch, and how I can help others. My role is to help people get jobs with Schusterman's grantees and partners. I also support my team with other leadership development initiatives such as a fellowship we run, executive leadership retreats, and other talent initiatives. The goal is still the same, to empower people's lives and help them live according to their values; however, the process feels different."

Lauren is a career coach who is creating change within a larger institution. Like Gayle, she is an intrapreneur. Part of the reason she finds her work meaningful is that she has surrounded herself with values-aligned peers. She works on a supportive team that shares a similar mission. This is one of the most important secrets to finding meaningful work. It's not only the institution you work for that matters. It's *who you work with* on a daily basis, and whether they see the world in a similar way as you.

Breakthrough Exercise: Community

Reflect on the following questions, either in writing or aloud:

In order to do your best work, what types of people do you want to surround yourself with?
What type of culture reflects your personality and your interests?
What are you looking for from your supervisor, from your team, and from your coworkers?

Part 6: Meaningful Work Is Financially Viable Given Your Desired Lifestyle

The final part of our "meaningful work" definition is finding work that is **financially viable** given your **desired lifestyle**. Many blog posts I read when I was thinking about quitting my job overlooked the small yet crucial detail of how the hell I was supposed to support myself once I leapt. They said, "Just go for it, follow your passion, don't worry about money!" I thought, does this person want me to jump from a moving airplane? Are they nuts?

That philosophy might work for early employees at Facebook, but I still owe Sallie Mae thousands of dollars in student loans, on top of rent, bills, and health care, so money is something I take very seriously. The advantage to worrying about money is that it made me a smart financial planner. I stayed in my job at least six months longer than I wanted to in order to save up enough money to avoid being a nervous wreck when I quit.

The downside of worrying about money is that it often keeps us from taking steps toward actually making money (finding a new job, starting a business, doing your work, selling your work). In the amount of time I've complained over the past three years about how hard it is to get paid well for freelance pieces, I probably could have written another book.

BALANCING MONEY AND MEANING

Whether you're self-employed or working for another organization (especially in an entry-level position), you may have to have multiple jobs and find more than one source of income to support yourself. In case you haven't checked your news feed recently: life is rough out there.

It is especially rough for writers. My friend Ryan Goldberg, a freelance journalist who often writes for *The New York Times*, has adapted to the changing economy. He says, "As for being an independent journalist, it's important in your early years to stay above water. You learn to live on less than most people; for me, I threw away the things that I couldn't afford anymore (eating at restaurants regularly, going to bars all the time). A lot of people take jobs outside the world of journalism to make money—such as tutoring, bartending, or waiting tables—while reporting the heck out of some quality stories. In my early years of freelancing, I supplemented my income by tutoring high school students in writing, and also moonlighting a few nights a week as a referee for a young professionals' dodgeball league.

"It was a grind, and often wore me down, but after a few years of writing quality stories and acquiring more and more assignments, I was able to drop those side gigs and focus all my energy on writing. Furthermore, I see my occupation as that of storyteller, and this opens me up to other, nonprint assignments—like television and film, both areas I've also worked in. You have to be flexible and also curious enough to try various assignments."

In between pitching stories to publications like *The New York Times*, *Men's Journal*, and Deadspin, Ryan has written copy for NBC's Olympics coverage, was an associate producer on ESPN's "30 for 30" documentary *Benji*, and worked on an Emmy Award–winning story for HBO's *Real Sports with Bryant Gumbel* (and has paid his bills)—all because he's remained flexible and been open to finding multiple income sources.

When you're considering new meaningful job opportunities, make sure that these positions provide you enough money to live the life you want to live. In order to keep his head above water as a freelance writer, Ryan was willing to make lifestyle sacrifices, like going out to dinner less often, that some people might not be willing to make. Remember that the journey is personal—we each have unique financial needs and responsibilities. Some of us have enormous student loans to pay off or health concerns. Some of us have children and some of us are taking care of families.

A good way to determine the cost of your desired lifestyle is to consider your estimated weekly and monthly expenses. This may include things like food, transportation, rent, utilities, and entertainment. Factor in loan payments, health care, and other bills you might have. Think about how much money you'd like to save each month for the future.

You might want to conduct a personal finance audit and start keeping a budget. There are free websites that help you track your expenses (like Mint.com) and others that provide more in-depth financial planning advice for a small cost (like LearnVest). Consider talking to an accountant and/or personal finance advisor if you're struggling with this.

WHAT IS YOUR BREAKTHROUGH PRIORITY?

In my experience, finding meaningful work is a never-ending balancing act. You have to balance each of these six parts and determine what your breakthrough priorities are. Your **breakthrough priority** is your bottom line, which says: *above all else, even if I have to make certain sacrifices, it's most important that my next lily pad allows me to* _____.

Is it more important to you that you get a job in your dream city or at your target organization? Is it more important that you're developing new skills or that you have a lot of autonomy at work? Is it more important that you do work you truly care about or make a lot of money?

In the two years after I left my federal job, I made about half as much money as when I worked for the government, but my life was infinitely more meaningful because I was doing work that made me come alive and I was living in a city I loved. This year, several years after quitting my government job, my business made about $70,000 from my writing and speaking—close to the same salary I had when I quit. Even though I obviously hope to earn more money in the future, I've found that pursuing a meaningful lifestyle is not about salary as much as it is about living in alignment with your purpose and priorities and surrounding yourself with supportive communities. An oft-cited Princeton University study showed that increased salary, after more than $75,000 annually, doesn't correlate to increased happiness or emotional well-being.

The breakthrough priorities we set for ourselves and the choices we make at a young age matter. Gayle and her husband, Ian, supported each other so they could prioritize raising their son, Emory, while still taking their careers seriously. If Ryan Allis's priority had only been wealth, he would have never started Hive, and five hundred leaders from sixty countries would never have experienced the Hive Global Leaders Program. If you value a job so much that you don't move to a new city with your partner, you may lose the person you love. If you put money over meaning, you may end up rich but unfulfilled.

I'll never forget a conversation I had with one of my older colleagues at the Peace Corps, not long after I first started. My colleague had been with the organization for almost ten years, was a senior manager, and was married with a family. I told her I didn't really like living in DC—the politics, the workaholics, and the humidity weren't for me—and that my dream since college was to live in San Francisco.

She told me that she and her husband had always wanted to leave DC when they were younger and move to a different place, but they got stuck because of her job. She mentioned that sometimes you have to make sacrifices in life, and that their priority had been job security over living in a place where they would have been more fulfilled. If she could do it all over again, she would have probably chosen fulfillment over job security, she told me. Her advice to me: based on my priorities, now was the time to take a risk; that the longer I stayed, the older I got, and the more life responsibilities I took on, the harder it was going to be to leave.

BREAKTHROUGH TAKEAWAYS

- To find meaningful work, figure out your *why*: why you wake up in the morning and what you want to do for the world. Reaching your potential means aligning your work with your purpose.
- In order to figure out what your purpose is now, examine your personality and your interests, how you want to share your gifts to help others, and what type of impact you want to make. In addition to being in line with this purpose, your next lily pad needs to provide a supportive community of believers, as well as enough money so that you can live a lifestyle that works for you.

Finding meaningful work is a never-ending balancing act. Always know what your breakthrough priorities are. What sacrifices are you willing to make? What sacrifices are you not willing to make?

CHAPTER 5

Find Alignment

"In 30 years maybe we'll look [backward], pretend like it all made sense along the way, and connect the dots into a beautiful narrative. But for now, I advise breaking it into smaller chunks. Is this next step right for me? Imagine the opportunity just one step after this one and see if it fits. But, also be ready to be surprised by life." —JANET FRISHBERG

THE ART OF trying to align your work with your purpose and balance your priorities in a constantly changing job market in the midst of a global recession (where 25 percent of twenty-five- to thirty-four-year-olds aren't employed!) is by no means easy. At times, alignment can feel close to impossible. But in the upcoming chapters, you'll learn how to beat the odds and make meaningful choices when it comes to putting your self-discovery work into practice during your job search.

A lot of people spend years searching in vain for the "perfect job." Accept the possibility that the perfect job might not exist for everyone, or that the perfect job at the age of twenty-two is different from the perfect job at the age of twenty-eight. Instead, let's adopt a new goal: to find a job or opportunity based on your purpose now that allows you to do four things*:

1. Share your gifts
2. Make a positive impact
3. Surround yourself with believers
4. Live your desired quality of life

* and pay rent!

Instead of looking for the perfect job, start your meaningful job search where many of your motivations overlap. Take your definition of meaningful work from the previous chapter, and turn it into an alignment Venn diagram showing **your gifts** (your personality, interests, and skills), the **impact** you want to have on the world, the **community** you want to surround yourself with, and your desired **quality of life**.

As you fill out your alignment Venn diagram, think about the overlapping circles: *What are your gifts that will get you paid and support your desired quality of life? How does the impact you want to have overlap with the types of people you want to surround yourself with?*

Once you've completed your alignment Venn diagram, put a check mark next to any of the things you're already honoring in your work today.

Alignment Venn Diagram

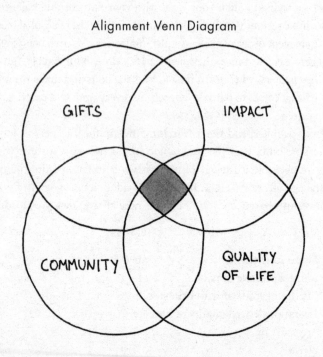

Smiley's Alignment Venn Diagram

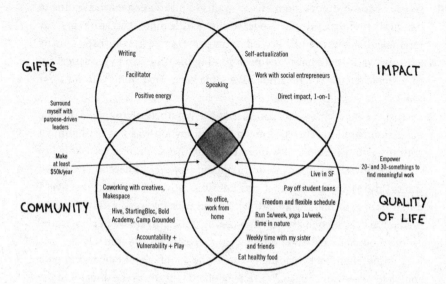

GIFTS

Writing

Facilitator

Speaking

Positive energy

Surround myself with purpose-driven leaders

Make at least $50k/year

IMPACT

Self-actualization

Work with social entrepreneurs

Direct impact, 1-on-1

Empower 20- and 30-somethings to find meaningful work

Live in SF

COMMUNITY

Coworking with creatives, Makespace

Hive, StartingBloc, Bold Academy, Camp Grounded

Accountability + Vulnerability + Play

No office, work from home

QUALITY OF LIFE

Pay off student loans

Freedom and flexible schedule

Run 5x/week, yoga 1x/week, time in nature

Weekly time with my sister and friends

Eat healthy food

Put a star next to any that you're not currently honoring but seem really important to you. Don't worry if your alignment Venn diagram is lacking a lot of check marks. Focus less on the check marks and more on the stars (what's really important to you), and refer to your alignment Venn diagram during your search for meaningful work.

ALIGNMENT TAKES TIME AND PATIENCE

Months after hoisting my hands in the air overlooking the Pacific Ocean, I finally embraced my fears to have "the talk" with my boss about leaving my job at the Peace Corps. Her response was that I should stay another year. Her rationale: employers really like to see that you worked for at least three years in every job.

While it's true that every employer wants to see a demonstrated track record of commitment (no manager wants to hire someone who's going to bail in six months), I decided to leave after a little more than two years. My rationale: I had learned all I could in my current role in two years. During a third year, I would have only been passing the time so a hypothetical future employer may or may not have said, *Well, good thing you did three years at the Peace Corps, you're hired.*

Instead of making a decision based on a hypothetical unknown, I made a decision based on current known factors: my job was not in alignment with my *gifts*, the *impact* I wanted to make, the *communities* I wanted to surround myself with, or my desired *quality of life*. I knew what I didn't want: I didn't want a job that was administrative rather than creative, I didn't want to be making an indirect impact with my work, I didn't want to pretend to be someone I wasn't by working unhealthy hours in a large government bureaucracy, and I didn't want to live in Washington, DC.

I found alignment by moving across the country and embarking on a completely new career path. When I got offered the job as the director of the Bold Academy, I knew it was the right fit for me because I could share my *gifts* to inspire others and show up every day as my positive, creative self. I knew I would be making the type of *impact* I wanted to make by encouraging others to reach their potential and supporting young entrepreneurs. And I knew that living in a *community* of creative people in the Bay Area, prioritizing work-life balance, and having time to spend on my personal writing would support my desired *quality of life*.

As you begin your search for the next lily pad to leap to, look for positions where you can share your unique gifts at organizations that match your values and provide the opportunity to make an impact, work with like-minded people who make you better, and support the quality of life you desire. In other words, find the sweet spot where as many of the pieces as possible overlap.

The alignment process—fitting these pieces together—takes time and patience. Sometimes it can feel imperfect or messy—and that's to be expected. I dislike delayed gratification as much as the next young person, but there's no "easy" button. Journalist Ryan Goldberg has been freelancing for more than eight years (and writing professionally for more than thirteen years). It wasn't until recently that he stopped refereeing dodgeball to help pay the bills.

Given the realities of the job market and your level of expertise, there may not be a position currently available that aligns exactly with what you're looking for or you may not be qualified for the position you want. Manage your expectations: if you're applying for your first job out of college or changing fields, you may not yet have the skills you need to get what you want. If that's the case, use the job-searching tactics detailed in chapter 7 to find a short-term apprenticeship or side project that will help you to get closer to where you want to be in the future. Remember, a breakthrough isn't about finding the perfect alignment overnight. It's simply about *finding a job or opportunity, based on your purpose now, that allows you to share your gifts, make a positive impact, surround yourself with believers, and live your desired quality of life.*

JANET FRISHBERG'S JOURNEY TO ALIGNMENT

Alignment can come from moving three thousand miles across the country like I did, or it can come from finding a work-life balance and new colleagues that energize you. A few years ago, Janet Frishberg, then twenty-four, was working for a workforce development nonprofit in San Francisco, helping job seekers write cover letters, draft résumés, and prepare for interviews. Although the work reflected her values, she found herself drained and needing a break from the nonprofit sector. As she remembers, "I was burned out and ready for a change of pace and to learn about a new world outside of nonprofits, which was where I'd been working since college. I also noticed that I was having a lot of trouble with work-life boundaries, emotionally; for instance, I'd go to sleep thinking about my clients and wake up thinking about them almost every day. This made it quite difficult to ever relax and to focus on my life outside of work, which was really important to me. I never felt like I could do enough."

Janet decided to leap to another lily pad. She leveraged the job-placement skills she had gained from three years at the nonprofit [*gifts*] and her interest in helping people find work [*impact*] with a job in technical recruiting at Airbnb. "I figured if I was changing sectors and industries, I might as well use some of the same skills so it'd be clear to employers how I'd be a fit," recalls Janet. "I was looking for a cohesive and collaborative team [*community*], a position where there'd be large opportunity for growth and professional development, and a company mission or product that I believed in. I wanted to feel like I could make a large impact but not be completely underwater every day, to find a company that viewed employees as humans rather than robots [*quality of life*]."

She found the transition to a completely new industry (tech) and a new sector (for-profit) invigorating. "I love my job at Airbnb," explains Janet. "Almost everything the company wants to do requires engineers, so it feels very relevant to be building out that team. I get a lot of gratification from the way we hire candidates, and I like how relational my daily work is. I believe in our process and enjoy helping people through the steps of evaluating whether this will be the best next move for them in their lives. Also, I adore my coworkers, both on my team and in the company in general. One of my favorite things is that I'm not seen as weird or disloyal for having passions outside of work. I work with people who are similarly passionate about Airbnb's mission, and who also spend their time deejaying or farming or screen printing or mentoring kids or bouldering or whatever they're into. I love that. More important, I can tell the people I work with genuinely care about me as a human being and are invested in my well-being and happiness, and I feel the same about them."

Janet finds meaning in working alongside her colleagues at Airbnb. Finding the right organization matters, but finding the right people to work with sometimes is even more important. "We laugh a lot throughout the day," she says. "I get really silly sometimes. It's probably the most myself at work that I've ever felt in a professional setting, which isn't a coincidence. There's a team of people working to ensure that we maintain a culture of authenticity in our office. It's energizing to be part of this collaborative, supportive unit of people."

In addition to being a technical recruiter on the university recruiting team at Airbnb, Janet is an extremely talented writer. She's currently working on finding a publisher for her first book, a memoir about grief that was sparked by the death of her good friend when she was seventeen. I first met Janet at a reading she gave for an anthology she had contributed to called *Get out of My Crotch: Twenty-One Writers Respond to America's War on Women's Rights and Reproductive Health.* I asked her why she didn't pursue her love for writing full-time and how she managed to find time to write her book with her nine-to-five job.

"Right now, I'm a better artist when I know how I'm going to pay my rent and buy my bus pass and all that," Janet told me. "I also know some people who feel like better artists when their income is dependent on their art because it forces them into action, and maybe one day I'll feel like that. For me, it's really great right now to not worry about where my income is coming from, because I've gotten really stressed about that in the past when I was having trouble supporting myself. Right now, I feel like I have the best of both worlds. I'm learning what I'm supposed to be learning from my paid work, while I also pursue my creative goals on a concurrent track."

Janet reminds all the writers and artists out there that you don't have to quit your job tomorrow to pursue something you love. As long as you figure out a way to make time for what you care about, there is no right way to pursue your art. "Writing is definitely one of my top priorities outside of work," says Janet. "I put it above certain kinds of socializing, I put it above partying, and sometimes I put it above exercising, unfortunately. So I have an expectation that I'll work on writing at least one evening during the week and one day each weekend. If I'm really on top of my stuff and getting enough sleep, I'll go to a café near my house before work for thirty or forty-five minutes and write in the morning."

In the last year, even with her full-time job, Janet has submitted numerous pieces to publications and writing fellowships. Ten of these pieces were published, and Janet got accepted into two writing workshops. She's learned that writing (like career fulfillment) isn't about overnight success. It's about being persistent as you take small steps in the right direction. "One of my pieces about suicide was rejected at least ten times before it was accepted," Janet says, "and once it was published I had so many people reach out to me to tell me how much it moved them or spoke to their experience. It just had to find its own home. As a recruiter I reject people all the time, so my relationship to being rejected is pretty low-key these days."

Embracing rejection is part of the journey. To help her keep going, Janet has found a support system of other writers and artists she can share her work with. She launched a writing adventure with her friend Caroline Kessler, called the 18 Somethings Project, which involves responding to a writing prompt for ten minutes each day for eighteen days straight, and sending your writing to another person, who responds to it with only positive feedback. Just like the community of support she has with her colleagues at Airbnb, Janet also has built a supportive community for her writing.

The last time we spoke, Janet was editing the final draft of her manuscript, and hustling to secure an agent and publisher for her memoir. Will she eventually decide to make the leap to being a full-time writer? She might. But one thing's for sure: whether or not she gets the book deal this time around (my guess is that she will because she's earned it), Janet will be persistent and keep pursuing her craft. By being flexible and mindful of her time, Janet has been able to balance her work at Airbnb and nurture her writing, a task that eludes many full-time writers I know. In pursuing alignment, she has found meaning, inside and outside of the workplace.

SERVE THE PEOPLE YOU LOVE

We often hear about people who turn something they love into a business, but we rarely hear how they actually do it. Let's take entrepreneur Nate Bagley as a case study in the challenges (and rewards) of launching your own venture to find alignment. Three years ago, Nate quit his corporate job to pursue something he had always dreamed of: creating the Loveumentary, a blog and podcast that shares stories of true love.

When he first started, Nate didn't even own a microphone to do his podcast, let alone have a vision for how his endeavor would make revenue. Interested in interviewing different kinds of couples (gay, straight, wealthy, poor, religious, married, polygamous, etc.) who were in happy relationships, he ran a Kickstarter campaign to fund a Loveumentary road trip. The Kickstarter campaign raised $30,000, and Nate's road trip ended up getting featured in *The Atlantic* and *Business Insider*. Nate ran an AMA (Ask Me Anything) about his experience that made it to the front page of Reddit. Making it to the front page of Reddit is akin to being the most popular thing on the Internet (more popular than Kanye West). Nate's AMA had over eight million subscribers; the traffic even crashed his website.

Nate still blogs and does podcast interviews, but his business has evolved into relationship coaching, speaking at workshops, and running a subscription service called Unbox Love. Unbox Love sends couples fun, creative dates in a box, designed to inspire romance, spontaneity, and love.

It has taken Nate more than three years to build his business into something that is making enough revenue to pay himself a salary. Three years is a long time. Most people cannot afford to go three years without income, and Nate is quick to admit that entrepreneurship is not for everyone. We often see our friends' entrepreneurial successes on our Facebook walls, but we rarely see their struggles or their failures. We hear about the large venture capital round or the *Fast Company* article, but we don't see the three years it takes to get there. I was curious about some of the sacrifices Nate's made while launching a company.

"I am now under constant pressure and stress to deliver for my customers and community," Nate told me. "The pressure never goes away. I've made many sacrifices to make Unbox Love a reality. One of them is living at home with my parents. I'm so lucky to have such supportive parents. Recently I learned that my mom has undergone criticism from some of her peers for allowing her thirty-one-year-old son to freeload in her basement. She's always believed in me and had faith that what I was doing would eventually produce results. Working on Unbox Love and the Loveumentary has meant not taking a salary for three years. I've burned through my life savings and incurred thousands of dollars of debt. I've missed out on vacations, dates with girls, bachelor parties, and other fun experiences because I was on a deadline or didn't have the money."

Nate's also had to learn a completely new industry. Before he started, he knew nothing about shipping, supply chain management, sourcing products, logistics, or business management. He had always been a creative. These analytical, process-driven, operations-based functions were way outside his comfort zone. "One of the biggest breakthroughs I've had in running my business was the moment I brought on people who were really good at doing the things that are my weaknesses," explains Nate. "Doing this has allowed me to focus more on my strengths, and I'm now seeing my business turn a corner."

Nate has learned the hard truth that entrepreneurs are not superheroes. They don't know everything. They have to weather ups and downs. It's not always easy, simple, or fun. I was curious if Nate thought his journey to alignment was worth it, given the sacrifices he's made. "Sometimes I wonder. Then I get an e-mail from a customer sharing the impact something I've created has had on their life, and I realize that it is so worth it.

"I remember once during a workshop, watching a couple that was obviously struggling. After every break they would go to the back of the room and whisper seriously to each other. It was clear they were trying to work something out. Toward the middle of the afternoon, we had a conversation about forgiveness. The couple was sitting in the front row. Suddenly, the wife reached over and whispered to her husband. I didn't catch all of it, but what I could hear were the words 'I'm sorry.' Instantly, they wrapped their arms around each other. The tension was gone. They spent the rest of the workshop cuddling."

I asked Nate if he thought all twentysomethings in search of meaning should turn their passion into a business. His response was blunt. "Absolutely not. I think everyone should have a passion project that they work on for joy and satisfaction. Making it a business can sometimes sully the project. When your love starts to feel like obligatory work, it's easy to lose the joy. Instead, serve the people you love. If it's the right fit, the opportunity will present itself for you to serve your community in exchange for money."

Nate gets meaning from helping his customers and making their relationships better. The alignment comes less from how he feels and more from the impact he's having on others. People always say, *Do what you love*, but I like Nate's philosophy better. *Serve the people you love.* Focus less on what makes you happy, and more on how you can make a positive contribution to others. When you approach your work from a point of service, it matters less whether you're running your own business from your parents' basement, or living three thousand miles away from your parents and working a full-time job. What's more important in determining alignment is whether you are offering your unique gifts to the world.

Alignment = Offering your unique contribution to the world

Nate has certainly struggled over the past three years, but he's discovering how to make his contribution (while acknowledging his weaknesses), and for that, all of us searching for love should be grateful.

STAY TRUE TO YOUR BREAKTHROUGH PRIORITIES

Alison Berman was living the twentysomething dream. Or rather, I should say, her grass on Facebook looked green. Really green. She was in her early twenties, living in a nice apartment in Manhattan, going out to trendy bars and restaurants, and working a well-paying job in marketing and business development at Rodale, Inc., a large publishing company. She had landed the job just two weeks after graduation, having completed an internship with Rodale during her spring semester senior year at Sarah Lawrence College. She then took a role as a marketing manager at Meredith Corporation, an even larger media company, and despite her move up the career ladder, she began to question what she was doing with her life.

"When I got into that role, some questions that were simmering quietly in the back of my mind flew to the front and essentially slapped me in the face," says Alison. "How did I get here? How did I build such a material-based life? If not this, then what? I enjoyed the financial independence I had, all of the intellectual stimulation I got from my social life outside of work, the exposure to new ideas, and the rigorous training I had been getting professionally. What wasn't working was that a whole chunk of me was completely missing from the picture: my love of the outdoors and long backcountry trips, my writing, and creative expression."

Alison became determined to transition out of marketing and publishing, leave New York City, practice her writing, and explore new directions for her career. She started a digital storytelling platform called Anchor & Leap, which chronicled her experience of what it was like to be at a crossroads in her career, and interviewed leaders and entrepreneurs in different fields about what they had learned about career fulfillment. Her website became an inspiration for her own journey, as well as a guide for other readers who were at an inflection point.

As we've seen, careers often do not move in straight lines, and we never know when the right (or wrong) opportunities are going to present themselves. *We constantly have to listen to the voice within and remind ourselves of what we want.*

Four months after quitting her marketing job, leaving New York City, and launching her website—just as Alison was about to move to San Francisco and transition into a career as a freelance writer—she got a job offer nearly too good to refuse, with a salary that paid $35,000 more than her previous job at Meredith. The trade-off? The job was to be a senior marketing manager for *Fast Company*, a major publishing company in New York. Alison would have to return to the very same life she had just rejected.

Working for *Fast Company* had been Alison's dream job for years, but it no longer fit her new career ambitions. Alison labored over the decision, but eventually decided to turn down the offer. Her rationale? "After my transition, I discovered that marketing was not the way I wanted to help the world, New York was not the city I wanted to live in, and publishing was not the industry I wanted to work in. Not accepting that job was one of the hardest decisions in my life, because it seemed absolutely crazy to turn it down. But turning down that job was absolutely critical to staying on my path and actualizing my true dreams."

Alison continued freelancing and moved to the Bay Area, where she could spend more of her free time doing outdoor activities she loved, like backpacking and surfing. A few months later, a new opportunity presented itself: to be a staff writer for Singularity University, an interdisciplinary graduate university, start-up accelerator, and think tank focused on exponentially growing technologies and their applications to positively impact billions of people. "Taking the job at Singularity University ended up being much easier than choosing to not accept the job in New York. After I got the offer and we nailed down all of the details, I realized I'd be able to retain the lifestyle I wanted, and simultaneously grow in the areas I was specifically looking to develop, and all the while be working with a company that I fully backed and wanted to get behind. When I slowed down, thought about the role, and turned inward to listen, it was a very clear yes that I should take the job."

Alison was clear on her breakthrough priorities. She knew she wanted to spend her days writing. She knew she didn't want to live in New York. She knew she wanted a lifestyle that provided more time to be outside in nature. She knew she wanted to work for a company that aligned with her interests. Alison navigated her journey to meaningful work by challenging her perceived limitations. She wasn't afraid to leave a lucrative job or hop off a career ladder she had climbed for several years, ever since her internship spring semester senior year of college. She wasn't afraid to try something new, even if it meant inventing her own path.

Alison turned her curiosity into hustle. Rather than wait for the opportunity to start writing, she simply started writing, creating her own platform and interviewing people who interested her. *When you hustle toward meaningful work, the universe conspires to support your efforts.* Before she got the job at Singularity, Alison showed her would-be boss her work on Anchor & Leap as an example of her writing style and narrative voice. Seeing her drive to launch and sustain such a quality website gave him confidence in Alison's work ethic. Without her hustle, Alison may never have landed the job at Singularity.

You can't judge a book by its cover, and you can't judge a twentysomething by their Facebook wall. While the last year of Alison's life probably looked a little messy on Facebook, compared to the early days of her career when she was enjoying the good life in New York City, it certainly has been more meaningful, and that's all that matters.

BREAKTHROUGH TAKEAWAYS

- A quarter-life breakthrough isn't about finding the perfect next step or answer, it's about finding an opportunity, based on your purpose right now, that allows you to share your gifts, make a positive impact, surround yourself with believers, and love your life.
- Instead of looking in vain for your dream job, start your meaningful job search where your **gifts**, the **impact** you want to have on the world, the **community** you want to surround yourself with, and your desired **quality of life** overlap. Be aware that you may not be able to address all four of these pieces at once, since finding meaningful work is a balancing act. Clarify your breakthrough priorities by asking yourself what's most important to you.

Alignment is not perfection, it's offering your unique contribution to the world.

CHAPTER 6

The Infinite Paths to Meaningful Work

"Try to keep your mind open to possibilities and your
mouth closed on matters that you don't know about.
Limit your 'always' and your 'nevers.'"
—AMY POEHLER

MOST BLOG POSTS and books about quitting your job to "do what you love" or "follow your dreams" mistakenly assume that everyone who seeks meaningful work wants to "go all in" by starting their own venture or becoming self-employed. While Tom started Rising Tide Car Wash because he was interested in ensuring people like his brother, who has autism, could find employment, and Nate started The Loveumentary to help people find love, not everyone who wants to make an impact is going to start a new business. If they did, who would work for Rising Tide Car Wash or the Loveumentary? Who would teach math to the fourth graders at Gayle's school or teach all the math teachers how to teach math?

This world needs breakthrough entrepreneurs as well as intrapreneurs (those working in companies, making change from the inside out). "Going all in" can involve starting your own venture, but it can also mean sharing your gifts by working for another organization, or splitting your time between getting your side project started and working part-time for a cause you believe in. "Going all in" is an indication of how much your work is aligned with your purpose, not whether you are your own boss.

There are advantages and disadvantages to starting your own venture, as well as pros and cons for working for someone else. In all cases, there'll be some trade-offs you have to make. You have to determine the right balance that provides meaning for you, as well as accept that this balance might change over time.

In this chapter, we'll explore all the ways having a job at an organization that matches your values can provide fulfillment. Contrary to what the blogs and my Facebook feed would have you believe, we'll learn a few important secrets about the path to meaningful work.

Seven Secrets About Meaningful Work the Blogosphere Will Never Tell You

1. The perfect job may not exist, but the right job does.
2. You don't have to quit your job tomorrow to find meaningful work—you can find meaning in your current job, and you can wait to quit your job as you save money and plan your breakthrough.
3. You don't have to be your own boss to find meaningful work.
4. You can pursue your artistic and creative passions while keeping a job that pays you well.
5. There are many advantages to working for a large organization, especially early in your career.
6. Working a job that's not the right fit will help you get closer to learning what *is* the right fit.
7. There is not one answer, rather infinite possible paths, when it comes to finding meaningful work.

ALIGN YOUR PERSONAL MISSION WITH AN ORGANIZATION'S MISSION

For Jon Leland, the years after college did not move in a straight line. Like many recent graduates—including myself—he wandered. Perhaps "wandering" doesn't quite fully capture it. Jon was all over the place. After graduating, he turned down a cushy job as marketing director of a company in Washington, DC, to become a busboy at a crappy restaurant in Bar Harbor, Maine (his words, not mine). Jon told me it was the best decision he ever made. In Maine, he got to know an alum from his school who was starting a nonprofit in South Africa, and Jon agreed to help her get it off the ground. The nonprofit, Thanda, provides education to orphans and vulnerable children whose lives have been marginalized by the HIV/AIDS epidemic. He spent the next three years moving around, building a computer lab and teaching a computer course for Thanda in South Africa, building freelance websites, and teaching the LSAT.

Upon returning from South Africa, Jon enrolled in law school at Stanford University, but quickly learned that he did not actually want to be a lawyer, and instead decided to start a tech company with a few other Stanford students. At the same time he was finishing law school and studying for the bar, he was building MyProject.is, a site that allowed people to use their network to help crowdsource ideas, information, and resources to help realize their projects.

"Once I saw the opportunity to create something to help people make things, that just became so much more compelling to me than being a lawyer," recalls Jon. "I had gone to law school in the first place because of the way of thinking that law schools value. In retrospect, it was a stupid thing to do. Starting a company after graduating instead of being a lawyer wasn't easy, to say the least. I graduated with more than $150,000 of debt and spent the first year racking up credit card debt, scraping by, and constantly worrying about my ability to keep myself and my company afloat financially.

"Eventually, as we continued to struggle with a core piece of the technology under the platform, I accepted an associate attorney position at a big law firm in Manhattan. That meant I also had to take the bar exam, while I still had the company in San Francisco. It was impossible. I was flying back and forth when I could, meeting potential investors at all hours, and working every moment. I wasn't fun and I wasn't healthy."

Many books that tell you to "do what you love" or "start the business of your dreams" don't tell you how hard it is to actually run a start-up. Jon and his cofounders discovered that running a business was too taxing on their bank accounts (and their sanity), and they couldn't afford to keep running MyProject.is. There wasn't a good option for selling the company, so Jon ended up taking a job offer from Kickstarter, a much larger start-up that, like MyProject.is, helps creatives make their dreams come true. In the last two years, he has worked as the director of community engagement and the director of strategy and insights, helping Kickstarter grow its community of creators and backers, developing strategies for international markets, and helping the company grow. Jon learned a hard truth most career advice books rarely teach you: *sometimes you can make more of a difference when you work for someone else.*

"The impact I have now is so much greater than the impact I had running my own start-up," Jon explains. "Honestly, the mythologized 'scrappiness' of being an entrepreneur in reality means being constantly focused on just keeping things afloat. Particularly when you have employees to take care of. Now I have a large role to play in helping shepherd the path of one of the world's most culturally impactful technology companies. Kickstarter is a small, independent company (120 people and founder controlled), so everyone's voice matters. I am learning more, worrying less, and serving the vision of my start-up better through my work at Kickstarter."

Think about that for a second. Jon is doing more for the vision of his start-up through working at Kickstarter than he was when he was actually running his own start-up. Rather than being preoccupied with getting featured on the cover of *Fast Company* and the coolness factor of being an entrepreneur, Jon is more focused on the impact he wants to have: helping creatives make their ideas become reality.

Jon's story reminds us that *it's okay to be a wanderer, provided you are wandering with intention.* We can't know exactly how our path is going to unfold. I'm sure if you told Jon when he was graduating college that he would spend the next ten years being a busboy at a restaurant, helping a nonprofit in South Africa, going to law school, starting a tech company, and then going to work for a tech company, he would have laughed in your face. But Jon listened to the voice within whenever it told him to jump to a new lily pad.

I asked Jon what advice he had for other twentysomething wanderers out there. "Don't become too attached to any picture of what success is going to look like in your life," he said. "Don't feel like you have to figure out *the thing* you should be doing with your life. Just find *a thing* to do for a time. It can be on the side; it does not have to be everything. Don't martyr yourself. It's good to have goals or a vision of where you want to be—it helps orient and motivate you on your journey. But as you go toward that vision, be very open to new paths and opportunities that open up along the way."

You don't have to know *the thing*. There may not even be one thing for you. What's more important is being open to making mistakes and course correcting when you do. When Jon realized that being a lawyer wasn't for him, he could have let failure overcome him—after all, he had made a three-year, $150,000 miscalculation. When he realized running a company also wasn't the right fit, he could have wallowed in failure again—he had spent countless hours and thousands of dollars on his start-up. Instead, he embraced his mistakes. He used these experiences as opportunities for growth and learning, getting closer and closer to what he was looking for. He embraced the journey.

FIND MEANING IN YOUR CURRENT JOB

Growing up in Los Angeles, Amira Polack always felt like she had something to prove. With a mom from a rural part of the Philippines, and a dad raised by a single mother in the Bronx, some of her teachers doubted her potential, telling her in high school, "wannabes like you don't get into schools like Princeton." Turns out they underestimated Amira's hustle.

At Princeton, Amira developed a passion for social entrepreneurship as a means to combat economic inequality and empower people around the world. During college, she launched her first social enterprise, Ubomi Beads, a small business that works with single mothers living in poverty in Cape Town, South Africa, to codesign and distribute beautiful, sustainable jewelry made from recycled magazines. Amira told me that the mothers she worked with on Ubomi taught her what it means to be an entrepreneur.

After college, she got a job as a social enterprise fellow at Hybrid Social Solutions, a ten-person start-up that distributes solar lanterns to rural villages in the Philippines, similar to the town where her mom grew up. Amira told me this experience was incredibly meaningful for her, since her mom grew up in a town that was mostly unelectrified, and hadn't been back for thirty years, since moving to the US to build a better life for her family.

At this point early in her career, Amira was faced with a decision. She could stay working in the Philippines, trying to scale a tiny social enterprise with minimal resources that was very important to her personal identity. Or she could get a job at a larger organization to invest in her business acumen. She decided that working for a larger organization would help her gain more formal business training so she could scale social enterprises in the future. "I looked to SAP because it's the world's leading enterprise software company," Amira told me. "It creates the technology that underpins the inner workings of the most impactful companies and organizations. I knew SAP would be a strong platform to develop my skills [and] global network and industry knowledge, to help me achieve my ultimate goal to make a difference."

Amira went from working in a garage with a handful of people with extremely scarce resources, trying to get solar lanterns to people in the most remote areas of the Philippines, to being one of seventy-five thousand employees in 130 countries working for SAP, a company that makes $17 billion a year and serves thousands of customers around the world. In the last two years at SAP, she has worked as a corporate social responsibility specialist, served as global head of the SAP Youth Campaign, and worked as a strategic relationships project manager.

"Getting to lead one of SAP's three global communications campaigns, especially around the topic of empowering youth (as a twenty-five-year-old myself), has been an incredible and rewarding experience," Amira explains. "I was shocked and humbled when our Global Corporate Affairs leadership appointed me to this role; typically, campaigns at this scale are run by very senior professionals. On a day-to-day basis, this role entailed coordinating a thirteen-person team based around the world, in places as far away as Singapore, Brussels, and Bogotá, to amplify signature SAP initiatives and partnerships around preparing youth for the future of work, including our Impactathon social innovation series with Net Impact, [Twitter] chats with youth in collaboration with Triple Pundit, as well as partnerships with TEDxTeen, We Are Family Foundation, and Africa Code Week."

Amira figured out a way to use the leverage of working at a large, resource-rich company to achieve her purpose of empowering those less fortunate. She certainly took a risk by leaving a social enterprise she was passionate about for a new lily pad, starting in an entry-level position for one of the world's largest companies, but Amira has been very intentional about how she's spent her time at SAP. She's pursued specific projects that match her values, sought out supportive supervisors, and done everything she can to make a positive impact with her work. As she describes, "Being in a position to be an intrapreneur means global exposure and impact in numbers many magnitudes of order greater than the vast, vast majority of other companies I could be at, let alone at a small social enterprise. My network and travel opportunities have grown explosively, and through SAP, I have met heads of state, Nobel Prize laureates, and CEOs of global companies."

She even nominated her former organization, Hybrid Social Solutions, to be one of SAP's Social Sabbatical candidates, which resulted in Hybrid receiving pro-bono consulting services. In this way, Amira has used her position at SAP to help distribute resources to causes she cares about most. It's hard to navigate a corporate job, especially when it's your first job out of college, or when you're at an early stage in your career. Amira's story helps illustrate a few ways millennial talent can pursue meaning within a large organization:

- **Know your why.** Knowing how your job fits into your larger purpose is crucial. Amira had an intention behind her work at SAP: she wanted to gain business skills as leverage to make a social impact. Knowing her why helped her become the global head of the SAP Youth Campaign, work on social innovation projects, and direct resources toward organizations like Hybrid Social Solutions.
- **Don't let your job title limit your hustle.** Be creative, challenge yourself to pursue new opportunities, and think beyond your pay grade. Amira never thought she would become the global head of the SAP Youth Campaign, but when the position presented itself, she jumped

on it, even if she was a little overwhelmed and had to learn new responsibilities on the job.

■ **Start young.** Amira didn't wait till graduation to start a business; she launched Ubomi Beads while she was still in college. It's never too early (or too late!) to explore your interests and start making an impact.

■ **Work abroad.** When Amira went to South Africa and the Philippines in her early twenties, she did not spend time hanging out on the beach enjoying the sunshine; instead, she contributed her gifts to the local community. There is nothing wrong with vacationing abroad, but working abroad sets you apart in a competitive job market. Amira's time working abroad helped her get closer to her purpose, which shaped her time at SAP and likely will continue to influence the rest of her career.

■ **Invest in your skills.** I meet a lot of entrepreneurs who are more concerned with calling themselves "founder" than they are with actually learning new business skills and gaining leverage that will aid their mission. Amira had to make a tough decision: while her work as the founder of Ubomi Beads, and then as a fellow for Hybrid Social Solutions in the Philippines, was incredibly meaningful for her, she realized that there was only so much she could learn from a small team working in a remote area of the Philippines. She discovered that the best way she could serve these people, as well as other marginalized populations, was by learning more. Her decision to work at SAP was an investment in her business skills and her future impact.

■ **Always add value before asking for favors.** Amira put in the extra effort and demonstrated a commitment to the issues she cared most about before gaining a promotion. She did her homework to find projects she wanted to work on and people she wanted to work with. The more you add value to your team and your organization, the more meaningful opportunities will come your way.

■ **Seek coleadership opportunities.** When I speak to Fortune 500 companies about how to empower millennial talent, I stress the importance of creating a collaborative relationship between young talent and more experienced talent. The goal is to allow new employees to learn from their colleagues with five to ten (or more) years of experience, while at the same time offering new talent the ability to step up and work on a project that is of paramount value to C-level executives. The assumption is that we millennials have a lot (read: A LOT) to learn from Gen-Xers and Boomers, and we also have something to teach them. Do everything you can to colead a project that matters to you and your organization.

- **You gain leverage when you do what you love at an organization where what you love is unique.** Most career advice books (including this one) tell you to find organizations that reflect your values and surround yourselves with like-minded individuals. This is definitely a great option for some people, like Jon (who sold his company and joined the team at Kickstarter because he wanted to surround himself with others passionate about crowdfunding). Also consider the alternative: doing something you love at an organization that isn't already doing what you love. SAP is a giant software company that is full of talented engineers and software developers but lacking young people passionate about social entrepreneurship and youth engagement. Amira's interests in those topics were unique and in high demand, and she likely had more opportunities at SAP than she would have working at a smaller social enterprise, where all her colleagues shared the same interests and talents.

- **Keep your work fresh and focused.** Commuting and working from the same desk every day can get boring. Switch it up. Ask your supervisor if you can work remotely every so often to change your routine. Take more breaks to go outside or exercise when you're at the office—if your supervisor has issues with this, send them research by the Energy Project and *Harvard Business Review*, which shows that employees who take a break every ninety minutes report a 30 percent higher level of focus, and employees who are able to focus on only one task at a time at work are 50 percent more engaged.

- **Don't wait for permission to find meaning in your current job.** If there's a project that aligns with your purpose, do it. If there's an initiative you want to be involved in, get involved. Few companies are completely void of meaningful work. If you wait for someone to give you meaningful work, you'll be waiting forever and get so bored you'll either fall asleep, or worse, start using Tinder at the office. Take initiative and make the ask to your supervisor.

Amira certainly accomplished her goal of jumping to a new lily pad to gain more business acumen, and along the way, she's managed to stay true to her purpose of using business to empower people around the world. She recently was offered a lucrative position at a venture-backed start-up in Silicon Valley, and got accepted to Harvard Business School. Amira is planning to defer B-school for at least a year, so she can keep learning and gaining work experience. I wonder what all her high school teachers who called her a "wannabe" are thinking now.

ARTISTS WITH FULL-TIME JOBS ARE STILL ARTISTS

We're often told we have to choose between "being an artist" and "working for the man." This is a false binary that makes a lot of young people feel they either have to be a starving artist (turning down a lucrative job that pays the bills and supports their desired lifestyle), or take the lucrative job that pays the bills (and ignore their artistic or creative passions).

Liz Flores is a talented painter who has spent most of her free time in the past year painting and drawing, completing over 150 new pieces. The first time I saw her work on Instagram, I felt like I was looking at a MoMA installation of what would happen if Pablo Picasso spent a few days on a road trip with Frida Kahlo.

The inspiration for Liz's recent creative burst came not in the studio but through travel, which she does for work in her job as a chief community manager for Under30Experiences, a travel company for young adults. Prior to this job, Liz also worked full-time on product implementation for a corporate contract company in Chicago. The job didn't interest Liz, and since she had to be there forty hours a week (along with working part-time for

Under30Experiences), she had little time to pursue her art. Liz realized she had to make a change and decided to quit her job at the contract company, while transitioning into a full-time role with Under30Experiences.

Liz's new situation provided far more alignment, allowing her to support her desired lifestyle and have time to paint. "Working for Under30Experiences has always been more than just work for me," says Liz. "Aside from painting, I love travel. It fuels my adventure, leads me to new sources of inspiration, and above all, I've grown the most wonderful community through traveling. After [I quit] my corporate position, my Under30Experiences job became more full-time. I handled community management, as well as operations and leading trips abroad. Having a separate job definitely gave me peace of mind when it came to finances and provided other avenues for me to tap into my artist in an experimental way. I was able to paint every day, while simultaneously working on projects aligned with values I believe in."

I find it interesting that Liz's newfound creative inspiration has coincided not with quitting her job and moving to an artist's shack in the woods, but with transitioning from a part-time role with one of her employers to a full-time role. As she started working more on projects that mattered to her, she painted more.

In addition to selling her own paintings and illustrations, her work has helped her meet a community of other artists committed to practicing and sharing their craft. She participated in the 100-Day Project, a celebration of process launched by Elle Luna, artist and author of *The Crossroads of Should and Must*. The project invites people from all over the world to participate in one hundred days of making, and share each piece on Instagram using a unique hashtag. Empowered by the accountability of sharing her work daily on social media (and getting over her fear of showing her work to strangers), Liz gave herself the space to play and not take her work so seriously. She also became Chicago's ambassador for the World We Want, a collective art movement and interactive chalkboard installation started by artist Amber Rae, with the mission to spark meaningful dialogue in communities across the globe, around a question many people are never asked: what world do you want to live in?

Liz's story shows that finding meaning is less about following your passion and more about ensuring that your work life *honors* your passions. "People often feel they don't have time to work a full-time job and honor their gifts," Liz told me. "I think what people fail to see is that honoring your passion doesn't have to mean spending hours in a studio after work. Or quitting your job. Following your passion simply means doing one small action every day that honors who you are."

Several months after moving into a full-time role with Under30Experiences, Liz decided to leave the company to focus 100 percent of her time on her art. Instead of thinking of your nine-to-five job and being an artist as separate pursuits you have to choose between, why not ask how your current job (or prospective job) can support your journey of honoring what you love and what you're good at? If your current job doesn't provide the time or energy to pursue something you care about, then you can make an adjustment, just like Liz did when she went from working full-time at a contract company, to working full-time at a travel company, to working full-time for herself.

Our work lives might seem messy when we explain them to our parents, or try to answer the requisite *So, what do you do?* at happy hour. Increasingly, the lines between "part-time" and "full-time" work are disappearing. By 2020, 40 percent of the US workforce (some sixty million people) will be freelancers or independent contractors. Liz spent less time worrying about whether she was a "part-time" or "full-time" artist, and more time making her unique contribution as an artist, which is all that matters.

QUIT YOUR JOB WITH INTENTION

You have to invent your own path, but Liz reminds us that you don't have to quit your job to honor your passions. However, if your current job is not in alignment with your purpose, you might have to make a big leap. Quitting my job and moving across the country from Washington, DC, to San Francisco was an essential stepping-stone in my breakthrough. But, unlike many career advice books, I don't recommend quitting your job tomorrow. Why? Because I didn't quit my job overnight! I stayed on at my job for six months longer than I wanted to, in order to save money so that I wouldn't go crazy when I got to California.

A lot of young people I meet are eager to act like Scarface from the movie *Half Baked*, who, when he quits his job at a burger joint, tells off his coworkers loudly and crassly. Please don't do that. Instead of quitting your job tomorrow and waking up the next morning full of regret, I recommend being more strategic about the process. If you need to leave your current job, that's great, but leave with intention. Here are a few questions to consider as you plan your exit:

1. Do I have enough money saved up to live my desired quality of life?
2. Do I know the lily pad I'm jumping to next? Do I have another job lined up?
3. What is the intention behind quitting my job? What is my definition of meaningful work that I'm striving for in my next opportunity?
4. What skills can I master in my current position that I can use as leverage for my next role? (Think back to the example of Janet, who quit her job at a nonprofit but used the job placement skills she had acquired there to land a recruiting job at Airbnb.)
5. Are my current boss and coworkers potential allies who can help my breakthrough? Are they believers who can support me moving forward? Do they have contacts that can help me find a job I really care about?

Remember, you don't have to quit your job tomorrow. Figure out what is most strategic given your personal circumstances and priorities.

EXPLORE AND INNOVATE WITHIN CONSTRAINTS

Sometimes the career path you've chosen requires doing a few tasks you don't want to do. News flash: there is a part of every job that sucks. Remember, we're talking about how to find meaningful *work*, not how to take a meaningful vacation. I love public speaking, but part of my speaking business involves sales. I hate sales. I have to put together media kits and flyers, brag about how great I am, and sell myself as a motivational speaker to colleges and companies. It sometimes makes me feel like Greg Kinnear's character in *Little Miss Sunshine*, trying to sell some made-up nine-step plan to success. I don't like selling myself, but I do it in order to earn the reward: speaking in front of an audience and helping people build careers that matter, which I very much enjoy.

Wren Elhai faces a lot of challenges at work. Four years ago, after working at a foreign policy think tank in Washington, DC, Wren joined the Foreign Service. There aren't too many jobs for twenty-five-year-olds trying to break into foreign policy, and the Foreign Service seemed like the best option for future growth. Wren has spent the last three years living in Russia, Pakistan, and Washington, DC. A lot of his work is bureaucratic in nature: writing memos, helping his boss with administrative duties, improving customer service processes for visa applicants. It's not exactly what young people think of when they think of the Foreign Service: Wren isn't advising the secretary of state; he's not on the front page of *The New York Times*.

Despite these constraints, Wren has discovered how to make his work matter. "I do the things I have to do as quickly as possible, to leave time to think and plan," Wren explains. "I draw motivation from identifying ways great and small that I can leave a mark and nudge the system in the right direction. In Karachi, I found those in interactions with individuals. Even if I was not changing US policy toward Pakistan in a significant way, I could make sure the people I met with, some of whom were marginalized and threatened, felt heard by the US government. I could show my respect for the local culture in ways that people found quite meaningful.

"A rigid system like the Foreign Service certainly constrains your options, frustratingly so at times. Sometimes, you feel swallowed up in the bureaucracy. However, if you have a sense of adventure, a willingness to adapt to other cultures, and the patience to keep nudging things in the right direction, the Foreign Service promises a meaningful career, and a truly meaningful life. Every couple of years, you get to seek new challenges, usually in a new country. It doesn't have the flatness of a start-up, but a limited menu of job options with progressively more responsibilities can be useful. Outside of the Foreign Service, I would not have set out to improve customer service for visa applicants or to understand the reasons for religious intolerance in Pakistan. I'm glad I got to explore those challenges and look forward to the next unexpected puzzle."

Millennials are quite fond of saying, *this job doesn't work for me, this job is too bureaucratic*, or *this job is too boring considering how awesome I am*. I'm not going to front—I've said many of those things, too. One of the reasons I left my job at the Peace Corps was because I felt like I was suffocating from all the bureaucracy. However, rather than complaining about how his job wasn't serving him, Wren figured out a way that he could thrive within the constraints of his job. *He was less concerned about what the job was or wasn't providing, and more focused on what he could give to his job, how he could make his own unique contribution.*

"I play a lot of music and have toyed with the notion of doing it full-time," Wren told me. "However, I spent the first several years of my career with a firm line in my head between my foreign policy wonk side and my musician side. Recently, I've learned to mix the two in rewarding ways. There aren't too many musician-diplomats out there, and I think I can be a better diplomat for having this other avenue to connect with people and create bonds. People appreciate my diplomatic reporting—they remember that I sang to them in their native tongue."

Even people who commit to long-term career paths, like the Foreign Service, medicine, law, or academia, have to remain flexible and keep exploring and adapting. Some of Wren's colleagues in the Foreign Service seek to climb the State Department's power ladder as quickly as possible, sometimes choosing jobs primarily for their value as stepping-stones. "It's a route I can see working, but it's not one I would enjoy," says Wren. "I'm trying to focus on taking jobs I'll find interesting, that offer me space for creativity and autonomy, and that I find impactful. A career is far too short to spend even 20 percent of it doing a job you don't find meaningful, in hopes that it will land you something better."

Joining the Foreign Service wasn't the last lily pad for Wren; in fact, it was just the next step in his ever-evolving journey. Even within a formal career path like the Foreign Service, Wren is constantly searching for new meaningful opportunities. Wren teaches us that if you want your career to matter, you have to explore within the constraints given to you. You have to make your career your own, even if that means becoming a musician-diplomat.

LEARNING WHAT'S *NOT* THE RIGHT FIT IS
JUST AS VALUABLE AS LEARNING WHAT IS

It's hard to know whether you're best suited to be an entrepreneur, or work for a larger organization, until you try one or the other and see what works best for you. Interestingly enough, Dorothy Zhuomei's path to a full-time coaching job came by way of a side hustle she was pursuing while working a full-time job she disliked. While getting her MBA at Northwestern University's Kellogg School of Management, she took a leadership coaching class, where she experienced the power of self-awareness and self-discovery work, and realized how much she enjoyed coaching her peers. However, Dorothy was getting her MBA with the intention to build up her résumé and gain credibility in the business community. Going into coaching post-MBA was almost unheard-of. So Dorothy did what many of her peers were doing: she decided to get a couple of years of management consulting experience.

Six months into her gig at a prestigious management consulting firm, Dorothy knew she didn't want to be a management consultant. "I was not feeling the impact of my work, and through my self-discovery at Kellogg, I knew that I needed to see impact on the individual level," Dorothy recalls. "I am not sure if I bought into the culture of management consulting, where you need to be very type A and do exactly what the firm needs you to do, even when the work is not aligned with your interests. I also didn't buy into the brutal consulting lifestyle. I wanted more control of my life. I knew I wanted something better, something that was more aligned with my values and mission in life."

Dorothy continued consulting for another six months, to save money and gain more experience. She started to pursue her love for coaching on the side, convincing the UCLA Anderson School of Management to build a peer coaching program, and participating in intensive weekend coaching workshops at Stanford. Eventually, Dorothy left her consulting job (which paid $150,000 a year) to pursue coaching full-time. Rather than go off on her own to build her own coaching practice, she got a full-time job as career coach at the Haas School of Business at UC Berkeley. I asked her why.

Dorothy replied, "I talked to a lot of people, mostly coaches, people in HR, other consultants in the people business, and found out that (1) coaching is a little bit of a 'white hair' industry where years of experience [matter]; (2) it takes time to build a coaching practice, and doing it slowly and on the side could reduce the anxiety and stress; (3) many coaches are affiliated with a firm, a group practice, or an institution, even when they are experienced.

"Combined with my own risk-tolerance level, and the cost of living in San Francisco, I knew that I wanted a full-time job that was somewhat aligned with what I want to do, and to explore my own coaching practice on the side. In the end, I was choosing between a senior HR manager role at a company, a leadership consultant role at a specialized consulting firm, and being a career coach at the Haas Business School. I chose Haas because it had the closest alignment with what I wanted to do, and it provided the most flexibility for me to explore my interests. It was the lowest-paying out of the three by far, so it was a bit of a hard choice."

Dorothy is now helping other MBAs pursue careers that align with their values, not just making money. I was curious whether she advised her students not to become management consultants, since the job had been so unfulfilling for her. "I don't necessarily think of my decision to go into consulting as a mistake," Dorothy said. "I believe that you are who you are because of your experience, and I learned a lot about myself, the work I am not aligned with, through my consulting experience. My work is about creating space for MBAs to develop more self-awareness. I think it is very important for them to reflect on their own values and what they want out of a career. I am less concerned or worried about their immediate job after business school, because I know that most people will switch jobs in the future, and it is really just the beginning of their journey. It is the life skills and mindset they develop that I care more about."

Every experience offers the opportunity to learn what matters to you, and what doesn't. Dorothy's career didn't end with her being a disgruntled management consultant; in fact, it was just the beginning of her journey to a new lily pad. Dorothy embraced the unknown. She fostered her interest in coaching, while playing it safe and getting a lucrative consulting job, and her side hustle eventually turned into a new meaningful career. Your first job out of college, or your first job out of business school, won't be your last. But it's a tremendous opportunity for self-discovery and growth.

WHO YOU WORK WITH MATTERS

Jon, Amira, Wren, and Dorothy are creating change within larger institutions. They are intrapreneurs. Part of the reason they find their work meaningful is that they have surrounded themselves with values-aligned peers, just like Janet found with her colleagues at Airbnb. They work on supportive teams with people who share a similar mission.

The institution you work for matters. Who you work with on a daily basis matters. Here's how Dorothy describes her relationship with her boss at Haas: "We both use coaching to develop people in a deeper way, beyond just helping them find the next job. Before joining Haas, I knew my manager valued me. Rather than manager and employee, we are colleagues. Our working style and skill set happen to complement each other, so I help him manage our team and our process, while he pushes our vision forward in the organization and provides me the space to experiment with my ideas. We are completely open in our communications. We went through the same coaching certification program, speak the same language, and work together as partners as we try to create change and impact at Haas."

If you're stuck in your search for fulfilling work, do what Dorothy did: seek colleagues who speak the same language as you, who truly understand where you're coming from.

Breakthrough Exercise: Finding Alignment in the Workplace

Here are several questions to ask when searching for alignment in the workplace:

1. Does my supervisor share my mission? Do the organization's core values reflect my purpose? Does this position allow me to share my *gifts*?

2. Will I make the *type of impact* I want to make? (Think back to the example of Gayle leaving the classroom but still continuing her work in education.)

3. Will my supervisor provide me the space to learn, experiment, and try all my ideas? Even if that means failing sometimes?

4. Is the *community* I'll be a part of (the size of the organization, the work environment, and the culture) the right fit for me? Will this community allow me to shine?

5. Do my colleagues share similar values about what matters most in life? Do we speak the same language? Will I be challenged by my boss and my colleagues? Can I learn something new from them, not just today, but six months from now?

6. Will this job allow me to be fulfilled outside of work? Will the salary and benefits support the *quality of life* I want for myself/my family? Will I have a healthy work-life balance? How long is the commute? Do I have to move far away from my partner or my close friends? Do I want to live in the city where the job is?

BREAKTHROUGH TAKEAWAYS

- There is not one answer, rather infinite possible paths when it comes to finding meaningful work. There are many advantages to working for a large organization, especially early in your career.
- Here are a few ways to find meaning at work: know your why, invest in your skills, don't let your job title limit your hustle, work abroad, explore within constraints, seek coleadership opportunities, keep your work fresh and focused, don't wait for permission, and seek like-minded colleagues.

It's okay to be a wanderer, provided you are wandering with intention. Every experience offers the opportunity to learn what matters to you, and what doesn't.

CHAPTER 7

How to Kick-Start Your Meaningful Job Search

*"Talk to everybody. Yeah, everybody. Even a
random biker on the street."*
—BERNAT FORTET UNANUE

DEFINING MEANINGFUL WORK and figuring out what alignment looks like
for you are crucial steps in the journey, and the next steps deal with applying this reflection to your job search in today's volatile job market.

Now that you have a better sense of what worked for people like Janet,
Nate, Alison, Amira, Jon, Liz, and Dorothy, and how to align potential
opportunities with your purpose, here are a few job search tactics you can
try out. The moral of this chapter is to worry less about your future job title,
and more about the journey itself. The journey does not happen overnight.
Every chance to share your ideas with the world is a worthwhile opportunity for learning and growth. Embracing your job search and being willing
to experiment and try new things will distinguish you from the crowd.

RAPID PROTOTYPE YOUR CAREER

Meaning isn't about doing what others are doing; it's about inventing your
own path. What works for someone else may not work for you. You have to
find your own way to the next lily pad, or in Amanda Zimmerman's case,
the next four lily pads.

When Amanda graduated from American University, the pressure to
follow the pack and get a job right out of college was brutal. "During the job
search I felt like I was running a race without knowing how far away the
finish line was," she said. "I spent the first month after graduation researching company after company and submitting cover letter after cover letter,

with almost no response." When her lease was up a month after graduation, Amanda did what many unemployed college graduates do: she moved back home with her parents. While she loves her parents, moving back home drained her motivation. She jumped on the first entry-level job offer she got, an executive assistant position at a marketing firm.

"For the first two months or so at the job, I was learning something new every day. From scheduling meetings for my boss and learning about our clients, to running our company social media, I was getting experience that felt new and exciting... until it no longer was new and exciting. Once I stopped learning, I started to realize that the work I was doing wasn't fulfilling my personal goals. I wanted to work with people and make an impact in some way. Every day I sat at my desk for hours, wondering about all the other things I could have been doing to make even the smallest difference in the world."

A few weeks later, everything changed for Amanda. She was having brunch with her college roommate, Stacey Levine, in New York City, telling her about how much she disliked her job, and a book she had been reading about how to find meaningful work. Stacey interrupted Amanda as she was eating her pancakes. "I know exactly what you have to do!" Stacey exclaimed. "You have to spend the next four months living in four cities, exploring all of your career interests!"

Amanda went back to Stacey's apartment and they spent the whole day planning her adventure. She decided that if she was going to feel confident about her journey, she'd need a bit of structure. She identified four interest areas (teaching and education reform, girls' empowerment, teen leadership development, and documentary film) that she would explore in New York, Austin, San Francisco, and Chicago, four cities she was interested in living in.

At first, Amanda's father was hesitant. Encouraging your daughter to quit her full-time job and travel for four months is not exactly what they advise parents to do in all those "how to raise your twentysomething" books. But once he saw that Amanda had a clear plan for how she was going to be spending her time productively, he was on board.

Amanda's journey allowed her to practice her writing skills, as she blogged weekly about the experience, and build her network of mentors and believers. In New York, she shadowed a friend who was teaching at a Success Academy charter school. She also attended an information session about the Future Project, a nonprofit that places dream directors in urban high schools, helping young people realize their potential. Learning more about the Future Project helped Amanda discover that she wanted to work with kids and teenagers on leadership development. "The only reason I hadn't come to this conclusion before," Amanda told me, "was because I didn't even know jobs existed that fit my interests."

In March, she went to Austin because of South by Southwest. She had always wanted to go to the festival, but tickets were so expensive. So Amanda volunteered, which allowed her to see films, go to comedy and music shows, and take advantage of the festival as much as possible. In San Francisco, she took an improv class, and was intentional about setting up meetings with people she admired: Dale Stephens (who started UnCollege), Jessica Semaan (founder of the Passion Co.), and Aminatou Sow (the podcaster behind Call Your Girlfriend and the cofounder of Tech LadyMafia).

In Chicago, Amanda found her first role model and mentor, the documentary filmmaker Dana Cook. Dana's documentary *The Empowerment Project* is about inspiring girls and women to conquer their fears. As part of her four-month journey, Amanda also volunteered at the Athena Film Festival, went to Creative Mornings lectures, attended events at General Assembly, went to Social Media Week, and volunteered at Art from the Streets, an organization in Austin that gives space and art supplies to the homeless so they can create art.

Amanda's "4 Months X 4 Cities" journey led her to more meaningful work than her previous job. She's now running a leadership development program for fourteen- to sixteen-year-olds at a summer camp. She's hoping this job will help her gain experience for future roles in leadership development and youth empowerment. I was curious if Amanda thinks every recent college graduate should do what she did, even if it meant quitting a job or burning through savings.

"I wouldn't recommend my specific journey to anyone," Amanda said. "I created '4 Months X 4 Cities' because it fit my needs and was a reflection of who I am as a person. I think if anyone tried to re-create it exactly, it wouldn't feel authentic. That doesn't mean that my journey can't inspire others. You can challenge yourself and put yourself in unfamiliar situations while staying in your current job and living in your current apartment (or even your parents' house). There are so many interesting people out there doing incredible things, and I'm willing to bet that more than a handful of them are within your reach. Tweet at someone you admire and ask to set up a Skype date, e-mail someone you have a shared connection with on LinkedIn and ask to pick their brain over coffee, start in your office and grab lunch with someone you've always wanted to get to know."

I didn't write about Amanda because I think you should spend the next four months living in New York, Austin, San Francisco, and Chicago (unless you want to—I kind of do). I wrote about Amanda because she reminds us, no matter where we live or what we're doing, that we have to spend the next four months *learning with intention*. You have to spend the next four months exploring your own career interests, researching organizations that interest you, going to events that excite you, volunteering at organizations, and reaching out to people you admire, like Amanda did with documentary filmmaker Dana Cook.

When Amanda graduated from college, she spent her days endlessly writing résumés and cover letters from her parents' house. She was productive in that she was applying for jobs, but she lacked an awareness of who she was or what she really wanted. Like most recent grads, she skipped a very important step in the process: asking the right questions. *Who am I? What do I want? What are my unique gifts? What do I want for the world? What types of people do I want to surround myself with? What is my purpose? Why am I here? Why?*

It was only when Amanda started 4 Months X 4 Cities, when she challenged herself to meet new people, explore new organizations, create new experiences, and embrace the unknown, that she began to answer these questions.

SEEK SHORT-TERM ENTRY-LEVEL EXPERIENCES

Amanda discovered what many young people discover when they work entry-level jobs that lack opportunities for learning and growth: it's hard to stay interested in a position when you've learned everything there is to know about the position after two months. It's crucial to find entry-level experiences that offer mentorship and apprenticeship, allowing you to learn from someone with expertise, someone with at least five more years of experience than you. You don't want day 154 of your job to be the exact same as day one; you want to learn something new every day.

Six months after graduating from college, when I moved to New York City to do freelance work in the film industry, like Amanda, I took any job I could get. For a few months I worked as a production assistant (or PA, as they're commonly referred to) on several different films. For one gig, my job was to sit on the back of the grip and electric truck, and make sure no one who wasn't part of the crew took anything (like lights or cables) from the truck.

For twelve hours a day, six days straight, in 20-degree weather, I sat on the back of a truck near Bryant Park and froze my butt off for $100 a day. Since the truck was a few blocks away from the set, I didn't learn anything about film production. I just sat on the back of a truck. I barely interacted with anyone, except for a few grips who chain-smoked all day and a few tourists who wandered by, asking if anyone famous was in the movie.

On my next gig, I worked for $50 a day as a PA on a small, independent film but told the line producer I didn't want to watch a truck, I wanted to be on set. Because the film was a low-budget project, they were highly understaffed, and I ended up becoming the assistant location manager, helping the location manager and the line producer scout new locations and manage on-set logistics for the film. I saw firsthand how involved making a movie really is.

While I got paid half as much, the experience of being an apprentice on set taught me infinitely more than making $100 a day guarding a truck.

Two months later, my location manager brought me onto another gig as her assistant location manager and paid me $200 a day. After that, I worked for nearly two years doing freelance location work. I learned so much that after two years of freelancing, I produced a short film about a day in the life of two Iraq War veterans struggling with posttraumatic stress disorder. Taking the skills I learned on various film sets, I managed a cast and crew of over forty people, something I never would have been able to do had I not turned the experience of getting frostbite on my toes into an opportunity for an apprenticeship.

Short-term entry-level experiences are important because they allow you to quickly test assumptions about your career interests. In four months, Amanda determined that she wanted to focus on leadership development for youth. In the same way companies use rapid prototyping to test new products and gain immediate user feedback, you can challenge your assumptions about how you might spend your days.

One of the pioneers of rapid prototyping in Silicon Valley is Tom Chi, who served as head of experience at Google X, and previously worked for Yahoo! and Microsoft. Tom and his colleagues came up with the first working prototype for the Google Glass using a coat hanger and a sheet protector that fourth graders use for book reports. It took them only one day—actually, forty-five minutes. Tom believes corporate cultures often stifle innovation. Decisions are not made by actually testing assumptions, but rather on ego. The person with the highest salary in the room usually gets to make all the decisions, even if that person doesn't have the best ideas.

Tom has been an astrophysics researcher (at the age of fifteen), a Fortune 500 consultant, and built software and hardware used by millions of people, as well as scaled social enterprises in the developing world. Rather than guess what his life purpose is, he is more focused on being a lifelong learner.

Like Tom and Amanda, treat your career like a lifelong experiment. Don't worry about finding the right answer; spend more time asking the right questions. Try new things, test assumptions, see what works for you, and learn what doesn't. Realizing that a specific job or sector or working environment is not the right fit for you is not a failure—it's essential data that will help you find meaning and fulfillment in the future.

Tom's mantra is to "maximize the rate of learning by minimizing the rate of time to try ideas." Rapid prototyping is all about learning as much as possible, as quickly as possible. People often spend days, months, even years talking about the changes they want to make. Stop talking. Start doing. Amanda and her friend Stacey probably would have kept having the same brunch conversation every Sunday, had Stacey not encouraged Amanda to pursue 4 Months X 4 Cities.

If you're new to a field, look for short-term, entry-level experiences in the form of apprenticeships, consulting opportunities, internships, or freelance gigs that offer on-the-ground learning and mentorship from people with expertise. While these experiences may pay less, they are much more valuable than entry-level jobs where you do something you already know how to do (like sit in the freezing cold and watch a truck, answer a phone, or schedule meetings). The best thing about short-term experiences is that if they aren't the right fit, you can easily move on to something else.

You won't find many entry-level experiences advertised on websites or job boards. You may have to create one for yourself, like Amanda did with 4 Months X 4 Cities, or when I asked my line producer if I could help out on set. If you're having trouble coming up with an idea for an apprenticeship, check out the Leap Year Project, created by Victor Saad. Interested in going to business school but worried about the cost, Victor created a self-directed, multicity master's degree in design, business development, and social innovation. He developed twelve different experiences in twelve months for himself, apprenticing with places like a leading architecture firm in Seattle, an art and apparel community in Chicago, and a digital agency in San Diego. Inspired by his leap year, he decided to create an actual school for others to learn by doing, called Experience Institute. Remember, it's possible to create any kind of short-term apprenticeship that makes sense for you.

LAUNCH A SIDE PROJECT

When I was writing my first book, I got stuck working on the second draft. I knew the first draft needed lots of work, but I faced a lot of resistance around actually sitting down and making revisions. Two months passed where I didn't work on the book at all.

All that changed one Monday evening when I went to my first Passion Co. class at my friend Jessica's apartment. I walked in the door and saw lots of smiling faces sitting on the floor on comfy turquoise meditation pillows, drinking spa water infused with fresh strawberries, eating Lebanese grape leaves and homemade flatbread topped with feta and za'atar, discussing their "passion projects."

By the end of the night, I'd made a commitment to my ten classmates that I would finish the second draft of my book in a month. It was an aggressive deadline, but something about being in an environment where other people were stepping outside their creative comfort zones and taking brave risks made me realize it was possible. I was given a "passion partner" to hold me accountable to my goal; we made a plan to call each other each week to check in. My passion partner even agreed to text me each morning at ten a.m. to make sure I was sitting down at my desk writing the second draft.

Now several years old, the Passion Co. has helped over six hundred people complete passion projects through their program, and expanded beyond San Francisco, with classes in Toronto, New York, Seattle, Beirut, and London. I knew I had to interview Passion Co. founder Jessica Semaan for this book. I wanted to know if she thought everyone who has a passion should turn it into a business. "At the Passion Co., we strongly advocate starting on the side, and only quitting your job when your side project becomes a sustainable business," Jessica told me. "Not all passions are businesses. There is a risk of losing your passion if you force it into a full-time business when you are not ready for it."

I was a little surprised at her answer. I figured the founder of a company called "The *Passion* Co." would be shouting *quit your job, follow your passion, and live happily after!* from the mountaintop. She wasn't. Jessica's own story reflected a different truth. She started the Passion Co. because she wasn't feeling fulfilled in her job at Airbnb. As Jessica explains, "I knew deep inside, since graduating from business school, that working for other people was not for me, and that one day I wanted to do something entrepreneurial."

"My first year at Airbnb was really exciting. I was tasked with an impossible mission to build a customer service team from fifteen people to 150 overnight. My manager at the time gave me a lot of decision-making independence and trusted me. Things started getting less exciting after that, when I was promoted to running customer service operations and having multiple direct reports. My job became highly operational, which is not what is meaningful to me. I am driven by innovation, self-expression, and starting and completing something."

Now, you might think someone as driven as Jessica, who graduated from one of the world's top business schools and was running customer service for one of the world's most successful tech start-ups, would quit her job at Airbnb the day she started being unhappy.

That's not what happened. Jessica began her journey to a new lily pad as a side project. While working a busy full-time job at Airbnb, she started a blog called Passion Stories, with the plan to interview a hundred people who were following their passions. After twenty interviews, it became clear that most of the people she was interviewing had launched their passion projects on the side, while maintaining full-time or part-time jobs.

Jessica decided to create an organization that helps people get started and take the first step toward exploring a personal project (creating a self-love ritual, beginning a meditation practice, learning to dance salsa), a creative pursuit (illustrating a cookbook, starting a blog, building a personal website), or a new business (becoming a floral designer, opening a restaurant, launching an online dating app). Most Passion Co. students do not end up quitting their jobs to turn their passions into a business, which is perfectly fine. But the process of committing to completing a passion project helps people realize what they value most, and helps them find more meaning in their current jobs, and in their lives outside of work as well.

Jessica herself ended up staying at her job at Airbnb for a year and a half after she taught her first class. A year and a half! We rarely see the behind-the-scenes efforts that go into starting a business. We see "quit your job and follow your passion" on Facebook, but we don't see that year and a half. Taking the time to interview a hundred people (while you have a full-time job) takes a lot of dedication and effort. If you are interested in starting a new business or honoring a creative passion of yours, don't expect it to happen overnight. Start like Jessica did: on the side. Start with research, not quitting your job and jumping off a mountaintop. Interview people who are doing what you want to be doing. "It takes time to build a brand and a trusted community," says Jessica. "Overnight success is rare, and expecting it to happen will lead to disappointment. Expect at least three years before your business takes off. It took Airbnb four years."

If it took Airbnb four years, it might take you a little longer. I don't say this to crush your dreams, but to help you realize them. To help you think of the journey to the next lily pad as an extended learning journey, not a like-able Facebook post. Too often we think of careers as strict definitions ("I am the director of customer experience at Airbnb"), and rarely as open-ended experiments in self-discovery ("I work as the director of customer experience at Airbnb *and* I'm launching a side project called the Passion Co., which helps people find and launch their passions").

Strict definitions lead to limiting beliefs. We think to ourselves, I work in customer experience, so how could I possibly make homemade flatbread and welcome people into my home for a workshop on finding your passion? *Open-ended experiments lead to possibility. You can become anyone you want to be.* Do what Jessica did: launch a side project.

FIRST, KNOW WHAT YOU WANT

People can't help you unless you know what you want.

I can't tell you how many e-mails I get from young professionals who are "looking for a job at an innovative company." What does that even mean? My guess is 99 percent of companies in the world would call themselves innovative. I have no idea how to help someone looking for a job at an innovative company. My response to these e-mails is usually, "Can you provide any more details about what you're looking for?"

In contrast, when someone e-mails asking for an introduction to someone in the design-for-social-good space, or wanting to meet someone with crowdfunding experience, or wanting to meet someone who works at a specific company, then I can help them. I can search my contacts and see if I know people who fit the specific parameters of their ask. Knowing what you want is not only a job-hunting tactic, it's a necessary life skill. When I organized a potluck picnic for my thirty-second birthday, I told people exactly what I wanted them to bring. Here's the e-mail I sent:

> Dear Friends: I turn thirty-two in a week, and nothing would make me happier than to celebrate the occasion with the people I love most. Please join me for a birthday picnic in the park on Sunday afternoon. As some of you know, I'm a yuppie hipster foodie snob, so don't let me catch you bringing some basic crap like Tostitos. :)
>
> WHAT TO BRING: Manchego cheese, chocolate chip cookies from Anthony's Cookies, fruit from the farmers' market, salt & pepper kettle chips, croissants from Tartine Bakery, pastrami from Wise Sons deli, pizza from Delfina, homemade guacamole, your favorite ginger beer, pie from Mission Pie, Izze sparkling sodas, Three Twins ice cream, those Dosa Chips that cost $13 for a two-ounce bag at Bi-Rite, homemade baked goods, dumplings from Kingdom of Dumpling, and brisket from 4505 Burgers & BBQ. I'll bring the bagels, lox, and cream cheese!

The first thing you can conclude from my e-mail is that, yes, San Francisco has turned me into a yuppie hipster foodie snob. I'm not afraid to admit it: I like delicious food. Don't hate. The only motivation I have for making more money in the future is so I can eat more delicious food.

The other thing you'll notice is that my e-mail is very specific. I included the exact items I wanted people to bring (from the stores I wanted people to buy them from). Guess what? Nearly every single delicacy on my list was at the picnic. It was the best birthday I've ever had. Most times you go to a picnic and the only food there is a bunch of chips and salsa, and if you're lucky, some hummus. Fifteen people come to the party, and ten of them bring bags of Tostitos. Not at my picnic. As my former roommate Natanya Biskar, a second-grade teacher, once observed, "Not being specific leads to mediocrity." Being specific leads to excellence. When you know what you want, people can help you get it.

MAKE THE ASK (EVEN ON A BICYCLE)

Many months ago, I was riding my bicycle through San Francisco's Mission District when a guy biked up next to me and started talking to me at a red light. He asked, "Hey, how was your day today, was it a hard day?"

I wondered, who's this crazy weirdo trying to talk to me? I pretty much ignored him, and as soon as the light turned green, I began biking faster, planning my escape route. The man started biking faster as well and kept talking to me. He told me his name was Bernat Fortet Unanue, and he had recently moved to San Francisco from Barcelona. Coincidentally, I had just returned from a vacation to Barcelona, visiting my best friend, who lived in the neighborhood where Bernat grew up.

We kept biking together for another fifteen minutes and talking. Bernat told me he had been job hunting for over a month with no luck. He explained that he was a user experience and user interface (UX/UI) designer— one of the best in Barcelona—and was on his way home from his third job interview of the day. He was desperately trying to find a job in San Francisco. He asked me what I was up to, and I told him that I was writing a book for people looking for meaningful work.

He said, "Do you have a cover designer yet?"

"No," I said. "Actually, I've been looking for one."

Bernat gave me his website, and when I got home, I checked it out. His work was amazing. We met again for tacos later that week, and I asked Bernat to design the cover of my first book. He said, "Of course!"

Knowing Bernat was still looking for work, I posted a link to Bernat's website on my Facebook wall, saying, "If anyone in the Bay Area is looking for an incredible UX/UI designer, you should talk to my buddy Bernat, he hails from Barcelona—and his work is incredible."

My friend Yee saw my Facebook post and commented, telling Bernat about an opportunity to work as the lead designer for his friend Mark's innovative mobile software start-up called Aviate in Palo Alto, California. Bernat met with Mark and the five-person Aviate team that week, and they hit it off. Two weeks later, he had a full-time, well-paid design job that sponsored his visa to work in the United States. And I had a beautiful book cover—all because he was crazy enough to talk to a stranger on his bike ride home.

About six months later, I got a text from Bernat that said, "I'm taking you out to dinner. You pick the restaurant, anywhere you want in the whole city."

I was like, Sweet! I'm a broke writer, I'd love to get taken out to dinner!

At dinner, Bernat told me the tiny start-up he'd joined (and had equity in), had just been acquired by Yahoo! for $80 million.

Bernat made the ask. He talked to a random stranger. On a bicycle. In a city he didn't live in. In a country he wasn't even from.

Take your job search beyond e-mail and social media and look for opportunities *everywhere*, even when you're biking down the street. The in-person connections you make will get you closer to where you want to go. The more specific your ask, the more likely others will be able to provide exactly what you're looking for.

I asked Bernat if he had any advice for other designers and creatives looking for jobs. "First, make stuff," he said. "Tons of stuff, really quickly. Make something cool every day. Second, cultivate your own opinion. Have a hypothesis of what you think is good and bad design. Talk to others, test your hypothesis, and critique it. Third, pursue many companies relentlessly. Ten interviews are better than five interviews. Fifty are better than ten. Talk to everybody. Yeah, everybody. Even a random biker on the street."

Smiley's Top Ten Meaningful Job Search Resources

1. **ReWork** (www.rework.jobs): Connects exceptional professionals with companies that are making the world a better place.
2. **50 Ways to Get a Job** (www.50waystogetajob.com): A website that offers actionable steps job seekers can take at every step in the process, from finding your purpose to interviewing for a job.
3. **B Lab** (www.bcorporation.net): A nonprofit dedicated to using the power of business to solve social and environmental problems. Provides a job board with open positions at B Corps.
4. **Escape the City** (www.escapethecity.org): A community of motivated corporate professionals who want to "do something different." Provides a job board with exciting, entrepreneurial, and impact-driven opportunities.
5. **GameChangers 500** (www.gamechangers500.com): Lists the world's top purpose-driven organizations and profiles organizations that are reinventing the rules of business around fun, fulfillment, and fairness to all life.
6. **80,000 Hours** (www.80000hours.org): UK-based organization that conducts research on careers with positive social impact and provides career advice, including guides and coaching.
7. **Imperative** (www.imperative.com): A personality test that helps you define your purpose and discover how to get the most out of your work.
8. **General Assembly** (www.generalassemb.ly): Offers classes from top practitioners of programming, business, and design. Courses are available in eight cities across the globe, as well as online.
9. **Experience Institute** (www.expinstitute.com): A twelve-month higher education program that partners with companies, creative workshops, and conferences to place students within real-world learning experiences.

10. **The Muse** (www.themuse.com): Offers exciting job opportunities, expert advice, and a peek behind the scenes into inspiring companies and career paths.

KNOW YOUR NONNEGOTIABLES

Usually, I do not recommend twentysomethings give away their services for free. My thinking is that if a company has revenue—if they can afford to buy coffee for the coffee machine—then they can also afford to pay you at least something. But there are exceptions to this rule. One of those exceptions is if you're a beginner looking to gain experience in an area where you have few skills. When I first started writing, I submitted my work to publications that don't pay their freelancers. When I first started speaking, I spoke anywhere and everywhere I could. None of those places paid me to speak, but they eventually led to well-paying opportunities, as you'll see in chapter 11.

Cesar Romero turned an unpaid role at Under30Experiences, which provides community-building travel experiences for young adults, into an opportunity for learning and growth. Unlike the traditional unpaid internship or entry-level job, where you get paid to answer the phone, set up chairs, and buy your boss coffee at Starbucks (tasks most fifteen-year-olds, let alone twenty-five-year-olds, can do), Cesar learned how to build a travel company. He traveled for ten months straight, leading trips in Costa Rica, Nicaragua, Iceland, and Peru. In remote places around the world, where participants were far away from their families and homes, he learned how to manage travel logistics, and witnessed firsthand what community building was about. Some people manage community from a Facebook page; Cesar was managing community from volcanoes and glaciers in Iceland.

Cesar's entry-level experience, while unpaid, was clearly worth his time. It led to a paid position with Under30Experiences, and helped him gain new skills. His job allowed him to easily visit his family in Nicaragua, and meet Jennifer (now his fiancée) on one of the trips.

A year later, Cesar started to get restless. The travel that he enjoyed so much when he first got the job started to become exhausting. He was also becoming more and more curious about what it would be like to take the experience he had gained from Under30Experiences and apply it to other organizations and projects. Cesar knew he needed to make a change. However, he didn't quit his job. Rather, he sat down with his supervisor and had an honest conversation. They agreed that Cesar could now choose which trips he would lead, leaving him more time to pursue freelance projects when he wasn't traveling. Cesar came up with a few "nonnegotiables" to determine which freelance projects he would pursue. Cesar told me his freelance projects must:

- Have a purpose he cares about
- Have a strong income potential
- Offer freedom and flexibility to set his own schedule
- Improve his leadership and digital marketing skills
- Allow him to be geographically independent
- Allow him to expand his network with other leaders and change makers

Whether you are looking for a job or a freelance project, it starts with knowing what you are looking for. These nonnegotiables are helping Cesar find several projects to make his breakthrough more engaging. He refers to his approach as "developing his portfolio of experiences." A portfolio is more dynamic than a résumé; you can pursue more than one project at a time.

STAND OUT FROM THE CROWD

In addition to using his nonnegotiables as a guide, Cesar is relying on personal connections, rather than online job postings, for his job search. "At first, I was looking at listings on websites and applying following the traditional route of submitting cover letters and résumés," explains Cesar. "I never heard back, and it turned into such a waste of time filling out applications, only to never hear anything. After months of getting nowhere, I decided it was time to switch my approach. I began reaching out to people in my network asking for introductions to companies doing meaningful work and job opportunities around community management, digital marketing, and business development."

Finding meaningful work requires going a step further than a normal job search. Sure, you need to do your usual homework: polish your résumé, find companies and positions that interest you, and conduct informational interviews. But the truth is, searching for a meaningful job on your own is an exercise in futility.

Because the competition is stiff, you need to "signal the noise," as my friend Sydney Malawer says. Once you know what you're looking for, recruit a cadre of supporters to find openings that might be a good fit for you. The more closely aligned your supporters are with your values and what you're looking for, the more likely they'll be able to connect you with the right job leads.

Cesar relied on his community, and the networks of people he had met while working for Under30Experiences, to find leads. Noticing that I was connected on LinkedIn to the CEO of one organization he was interested in working for, Cesar reached out to me, asking for an introduction. In his e-mail, Cesar didn't include a cover letter or résumé, but rather a link to a one-page website of his portfolio. I asked Cesar about his portfolio page. He created it using Strikingly, which allows you to create a simple, beautifully designed one-page portfolio website in less time than it takes to change the margins of a Microsoft Word doc.

"In my experience, traditional résumés and cover letters do not get results," Cesar explained. "The key is to get people's attention, and the only way to do that is to stand out. You can have your résumé and cover letter in a Word doc or PDF, that's fine. But you also need to create an 'out of the box' format to get people's attention. On my Strikingly page, I include pictures, text, and video that demonstrate not only my qualifications, but my work ethic, personality, and values."

Today's competitive job market rewards people who think outside the box, who don't define themselves by one position, and who don't market themselves using lots of boring words on a résumé. Cesar's approach has already led to a new community management project with Hive, which trains purpose-driven leaders. The role honors several of his nonnegotiables: it's a project he cares deeply about, and he can set his own schedule and work from anywhere, practice his digital marketing skills, and expand his network of purpose-driven leaders. He's also submitting a digital marketing proposal to another travel start-up for freelance work, and is in the process of revamping his portfolio website.

A lot of people complain that their job isn't perfect. Cesar knows his job isn't perfect. Cesar knows that nobody's job is perfect. Instead of complaining, he's starting to identify what he wants, taking tangible steps to find more meaning in his current job, and taking on freelance projects that excite him. He's building his portfolio of meaningful experiences, which will only help him on his journey.

Breakthrough Exercise: How to Create a Beautiful Portfolio Website in Ten Simple Steps

1. Go to Strikingly.com or Squarespace.com, and register the domain name for your personal website or portfolio page. I recommend using your first and last name (for example, my personal website is: smileyposwolsky.com).
2. Come up with a few words to describe who you are (for example, my website states: "Author. Speaker. Millennial.").
3. Upload a high-quality wide-angle photo of you that reflects your personality and your work. Make this photo your home page background.
4. Write a one-sentence mission statement that describes your current purpose (or what you're looking for in your job search). For example, my mission statement is: "I empower millennials to find meaningful work."
5. Add your professional bio and head shot.

6. Provide links to samples of your work (blog posts, videos, photographs, events, projects, etc.).
7. Add logos of companies where you've worked, or organizations you've collaborated with.
8. Add two to three testimonials (recommendations) of your work, from previous clients, supervisors, colleagues, professors, or mentors.
9. Add links to any press or awards you've received.
10. Add links to your LinkedIn, Twitter, blog, and any other professional social media profiles. Be sure to include your e-mail so potential job leads can reach you!

TEST YOUR IDEA: CROWDFUND YOUR PURPOSE PROJECT

As artists, we are rather harsh on ourselves. We tend to wait until the last moment, until our work is 100 percent "perfect," to share it with the world. Unlike product or software developers who revel in frequent beta testing and user experience research, we often treat our manuscripts, canvases, and studios as caves, and rarely emerge to ask the public if they even like what we're working on.

With my first book, I decided to be less a writer and more a tech entrepreneur like Tom Chi; I used crowdfunding as a practice launch for the book you're reading now. In 2013, I ran an Indiegogo campaign to raise money to self-publish the book, before I even finished writing the introduction. Running a crowdfunding campaign is a great way to test a new business idea. You learn how to be confident, put yourself out there, make the ask, build a website, manage a budget, create a business plan, market a product, and think about sales and customer service. I think I learned more from running a thirty-day crowdfunding campaign than I did from most of my classes in college. My Indiegogo campaign ended up raising nearly $13,000 (140 percent of my goal) from five hundred funders in forty countries, was shared 1,200 times on Facebook, and was featured on the Indiegogo home page as well as in *Fast Company* and *GOOD* magazine.

My crowdfunding campaign served as a stepping-stone for launching my first book, which was a stepping-stone for this book you're reading now. The journey does not happen overnight. Every opportunity to share your ideas with the world is a worthwhile opportunity for learning and growth. By treating my Indiegogo campaign as a beta launch and testing my product before it was finished, I learned two invaluable lessons:

Lesson 1: People wanted the book. The idea resonated; there was demand for my product. People I didn't even know were sharing it on Facebook. At least 50 percent of my five hundred backers were people I had never met before, from places like Lincoln, Nebraska; Bowling Green, Kentucky; Calgary, Alberta; and as far away as India, Portugal, and Iceland. People wrote comments on the Indiegogo page like, "This project lifted my spirits today," and "I need this book right now, can't wait to read it!"

Lesson 2: People didn't want the version of the book I had planned on writing. People were asking for more of a self-help book with practical exercises, and less of a personal memoir. In all my conversations, my funders wanted something different than my initial plan for the book. Knowing this while my book was still in development allowed me to make essential changes in my second draft that ended up increasing the book's impact (and future sales).

Remember: you don't have to quit your job tomorrow, the second you have a brilliant idea for a new project. Crowdfunding is a great way to test a business idea or even your next lily pad. Once you hear Debbie Sterling's story, you'll understand why.

Ten years ago, Debbie was one of very few women in her engineering major at Stanford University. During a three-dimensional drawing class, a male teaching assistant held up one of Debbie's drawings in front of everyone and asked, "Who else thinks Debbie should fail this assignment, and why?"

Debbie remembers, "It was so messed up. I cried in the bathroom. It was one of the most embarrassing moments of my life. I knew I could do the drawing, I just needed the foundation, the spatial training they weren't providing. I lacked confidence after that, and I understood why so many women stayed away from engineering."

Women have historically been represented at far lower rates than men in science and engineering, both professionally and in college programs. A mere 5 percent of first-year female college students intend to major in science, technology, engineering, and mathematics (STEM) fields, and only about 10 percent of engineers in the US workforce are women.

After college, Debbie moved away from engineering and interned at a graphic design company in Seattle. Seeking more meaningful work, she volunteered in rural India with the British volunteer organization VSO. When she moved back to San Francisco with her husband, she found a job via LinkedIn as the marketing director of a jewelry company. She had enjoyed making jewelry in college and was convinced jewelry was her "calling."

After a year, though, Debbie grew tired of working in the jewelry industry and became re-interested in what she had studied in college: engineering. With her own embarrassing experience from Stanford imprinted upon her memory, she had an idea for a company that would create more opportunities for female engineers. While out one Sunday eating pancakes at brunch, Debbie's friend, another female engineer from Stanford, told the group that she'd gotten interested in the field by playing with her older brother's hand-me-down construction toys. If only there were construction toys designed for girls! The moment this idea struck, Debbie knew it was her life mission: start a toy company to get young girls interested in engineering.

Her friends loved the idea and told her she had to pursue it. From the living room of her small apartment in San Francisco, Debbie created GoldieBlox, a construction set and companion storybook designed specifically for the way young girls learn. The toy helps girls learn spatial skills by leveraging their verbal skills. Debbie's goal was to level the playing field with boys, who learn spatial skills throughout their childhood from a variety of toys like LEGOs, Bob the Builder, and Thomas the Tank Engine.

She started prototyping the toy on nights and weekends, and stayed on at the jewelry company for another nine months. Let me repeat that: she didn't quit her job overnight—she stayed on for another nine months. Why? For starters, she wanted to save money. More important, though, she was gaining valuable skills in marketing, financial planning, sales, retail shipping, and distribution—expertise that she knew would come in handy when launching her own business. As she told me, "I didn't quit my job right away; I treated my job as training for what I knew I was going to do next. I felt like I was getting paid to go to business school."

To test out her idea, Debbie turned to crowdfunding, funding the first GoldieBlox production run with a Kickstarter campaign that raised over $285,000 from fifty-five hundred backers. Her toy was featured in *The Atlantic*, on Upworthy, and on *Good Morning America*. It became a huge hit at Toy Fair and Maker Faire, and it's now sold at Walmart, Barnes & Noble, and Toys "R" Us stores across the country. A GoldieBlox ad ran during the 2014 Super Bowl, and GoldieBlox videos have over twenty million views on YouTube. It turns out a whole lot of other people shared Debbie's belief that if women make up half the population, they should also be the ones designing and building the things we use every day.

Eventually, Debbie did leave her job to work on GoldieBlox full-time. She started telling more people about her idea, and the enthusiasm was palpable, so much so that several friends started working for her.

GoldieBlox did not end up on the shelves of the largest toy stores in the world overnight. It got there because when Debbie was still working full-time for a jewelry company, she became obsessed with an incomplete and imperfect idea with friends over pancakes. Debbie was willing to put herself out there, and test her new business through a crowdfunding campaign. Her idea clearly resonated, and people came flocking to support her and her vision.

BREAKTHROUGH TAKEAWAYS

- Meaning isn't about doing what others are doing; it's about inventing your own path. Embracing your job search and becoming willing to experiment and try new things will distinguish you from the crowd.
- Apply the principles of rapid prototyping to your career. Try new things, test assumptions, see what works for you, and learn what doesn't. Short-term entry-level experiences, side projects, and crowdfunding campaigns allow you to quickly test assumptions about your career interests.

When you know what you want, people can help you get it. First, know your nonnegotiables. Then, be willing to put yourself out there and make the ask.

CHAPTER 8

Is Graduate School Worth It?

*"Your time is limited, so don't waste it
living someone else's life."*
—STEVE JOBS

DURING A QUARTER-LIFE transition, many people face the question of whether to pursue graduate school. There have been countless times over the past ten years that I've been in a bookstore and come *this* close to buying a GRE study guide. But even though grad school has seemed attractive to me at various times during my twenties because I love learning so much, I've never actually taken the GRE or applied to a master's program. This is mostly because the idea of accumulating more debt terrifies me, and partly because I've been interested in so many different things that I never felt committed to pursuing any one degree in particular.

However, I have many friends who have pursued graduate degrees in law, business, medicine, public policy, and environmental management, among others. For some, grad school has been a life-changing breakthrough. For others, it was a costly decision they now regret. The stories in this chapter will help you determine whether grad school makes sense in the context of your breakthrough.

DON'T GO TO LAW SCHOOL TO ANSWER THE REQUISITE HAPPY-HOUR QUESTION: "WHAT THE HELL ARE YOU DOING WITH YOUR LIFE?" (GO TO LAW SCHOOL WITH INTENTION)

I have a thirty-two-year-old friend named "Kate" who recently finished law school, passed the bar, and is now making over $150,000 a year (plus bonuses) as a junior associate for a large, prestigious corporate law firm. Not long ago, Kate and I had dinner and she told me, "I wish I had known what

I wanted to do before I went to law school, because I knew I wasn't passionate about the law or practicing law. I made a practical decision—I wanted future stability and financial flexibility."

She told me that she had worked till one o'clock in the morning four nights in a row that week, and she was miserable at work. She also mentioned that after a year of studying for the LSAT and applying to law school, three years of law school, hundreds of thousands of dollars of tuition, and a year at her firm, she'd recently had a realization that she wanted to brighten people's lives by becoming an interior decorator.

After talking to so many people who went to graduate school for different degrees, I've determined that there are two main groups that people fall into, in terms of why they want to go to grad school. In one group, you have folks who want to learn a new skill set, meet inspiring people who share common interests, and use the degree as a means to align their work with their purpose. In another group, you have people who go to grad school because they don't know what they want to do, are scared to ask themselves what they actually want, and want to make money when they're older and easily be able to answer the question "So what are your plans now?"

In other words, there are *people who have a clear intention behind why they are going to grad school and people who don't*.

Beyond wanting an intellectual challenge, Kate didn't really know *why* she went to law school. On the other hand, Conor Gleason, another thirty-two-year-old lawyer friend of mine, pursued law school as a means to an end, inspired by his desire to help people who are marginalized in society. After finishing his undergraduate degree, he spent a year volunteering in a poor community in Ecuador as an English teacher and after-school program coordinator. He went on to work as an investigator at a public defense office for almost three years in New York, helping gather information to defend people accused of crimes.

Conor's interest in law school was inspired by his unique job experiences following college. "I recognized that my capacity to make change and fight for social justice was hampered by my minimal skill set," explains Conor. "A law degree meant more skills, which equated to more opportunity to make change." After attending law school, Conor passed the New York bar, and started working as an immigration attorney for the Bronx Defenders, a public defense office that provides innovative and client-centered criminal defense, family defense, civil legal services, social work support, and advocacy to indigent people of the Bronx.

Conor recently defended a longtime lawful permanent resident from being deported. He explains, "Congress decided almost two decades ago that people convicted of certain crimes—including many nonviolent misdemeanors—cannot get bond in immigration proceedings and must remain in detention throughout the course of their case. Our client was in mandatory detention for almost a year while we fought the case; there was essentially nothing we could do to get him out."

After almost a year of hard work, Conor and his colleagues won their case and freed their client from detention. The resident is now back in the United States, reunited with his fiancée and his daughter, both US citizens. "Seeing him out of detention and in street clothes for the first time was amazing. The hug we exchanged was something I will never forget," Conor said.

Though Conor certainly finds his work meaningful, it has been an uphill battle. Unlike some of his classmates, who were making well over six figures at corporate firms, Conor started off making about $50,000 a year, and he was in $185,000 of debt upon graduation from law school. If you think it's hard to work with purpose, try working with purpose when you have $185,000 of student loans to pay off. However, when I asked Conor whether he felt law school was worth it as a means to an end, he told me absolutely it was.

"So many of my clients—immigrants and people of color—are marginalized by the justice system. It is an honor to work with them and combat those injustices, and even if it's rare, win a bit of justice for our clients. I know too much about how low-income black and brown people are treated in our society by the police, the courts, and law enforcement, to not try and fight it every day. Yes, my job is taxing, and the reality facing my clients makes certain days difficult. But knowing what I know, I would not be able to get out of bed in the morning and do something different."

As part of his work with the Bronx Defenders, Conor was one of the first four attorneys who helped launch the New York Immigrant Family Unity Project, the first-ever public defender system in the United States for immigrants facing deportation. NYIFUP provides free, high-quality legal representation to every poor immigrant facing deportation in New York City. The program now has over thirty attorneys and support staff.

"I think law school is 'worth it' for anybody who is dedicated to learning and gaining insight into how our public institutions and social structures function," Conor said. "Law school is very hard. It is time-consuming, draining, and it changes your daily life completely. Public interest students face similar pressures as students going the corporate route—there is a tremendous amount of stress and competition in law school, no matter where you go and no matter your goals. You are graded on a curve, and you are ranked—most jobs consider your ranking, where you went to law school, and your experience. Thus, it makes the grueling three years—plus the brutal misery that is studying for the bar—pass by a lot more smoothly if you have a long-term goal in sight."

ONLY GO TO GRAD SCHOOL IF YOU CAN'T NOT GO

Provided you have a clear purpose like Conor did, grad school can make sense. This doesn't necessarily mean you have to want to stay in the field of your degree for the rest of your life. Conor mentioned that several of his classmates are now working in education or social enterprise, or for tech start-ups. But it does mean you should think deeply about whether grad school will enable your mission and how debt will affect your ability to live your desired lifestyle in the near future. The years of living abroad in Ecuador and working as an investigator allowed Conor to discover his commitment to social justice and learn why he wanted to go to law school. Had he gone to law school at the age of twenty-three, he might not have found the degree as useful.

I meet a lot of recent college graduates who feel pressure to go to grad school in their early twenties. I advise against going back to school until you are 100 percent ready and the degree is essential for your next lily pad.

Lindsey Franklin decided to attend divinity school eight years after graduating from college. Her story proves that the years you spend experimenting and gaining work experience often point you in the direction of what you want to study. Those who go to grad school at twenty-three because they don't know how to answer the requisite happy-hour question *So, what are you doing with your life?* don't end up fulfilled, they end up unemployed and in lots of debt.

Lindsey has spent the last eight years connecting communities of people and driving social and political change. She began her career as a climate activist and political organizer, and most recently spent three years working as a program manager for New Media Ventures, an investor network focused on funding progressive media and technology start-ups like Upworthy, Daily Kos, SumOfUs, and NationalField. The job was a great fit for her because it combined her passion for politics with her skills in community building, while developing her understanding of the start-up world. For three years, she helped build a network of activists, investors, and entrepreneurs supporting companies that use the Internet to drive progressive political change.

While Lindsey loved her job at New Media Ventures, there was a part of her that was still unsatisfied. Lindsey started to realize that she wanted her work building communities to go deeper than connecting individuals and organizations to funders. Around the same time, she was searching for a church in San Francisco that could fill the spiritual void she felt in her life. "While I don't quite identify as Christian," Lindsey explains, "I grew up in the Congregational Church, under the umbrella of the United Church of Christ—a church that is both theologically and socially progressive. I missed the weekly spiritual and ethical pause that church gives, and the community of support and sense of place it offers.

"I started to think about the idea of going back to school," Lindsey told me. "I knew that I wanted to work leading groups of people, connecting them to one another toward a common goal. When thinking about grad school, I could see myself doing just that in business or politics, so I considered both business and public policy school. But I kept hearing this lingering voice in my head to consider divinity school. I had studied religion and philosophy in college, and I absolutely love ethics, so I always thought of divinity school as something I would do in another life. Then I thought, what about in this life?

"That's when it hit me, quite powerfully: I wanted to be a minister. I believe that ministry is the essential missing ingredient to the communities I want to build in my life—radically diverse groups of people who come together with their whole selves, capable of creating deep connections and lasting social change. And while I will certainly be an unconventional minister, and may find myself far outside traditional institutions, I want to learn the art and skills of ministry."

Our generation has witnessed a severe decline in church membership (across religious institutions), and Lindsey is now on a mission to provide a sense of place and community to her peers. A year ago, she was entrenched in the cutthroat world that is start-up venture capital in Silicon Valley. This year, she's attending Harvard Divinity School. Is Lindsey nervous about her new lily pad? Of course she is. Divinity school isn't exactly a sure ticket to a high-paying job.

"I know I am taking a financial risk with this decision," Lindsey told me. "I am headed down a path of very murky financial gain. Even the most successful ministers don't make much money (unless they are televangelists or megachurch pastors, neither of which I will become). But I am lucky, and grateful, to have a strong financial safety net in that I come from a privileged background. While I have to figure out how to make my life financially sustainable, I also know that in the worst-case scenario, my family could support me. The risk I am taking is different from others who have more at stake financially."

In the process of making this decision, Lindsey has learned a few important lessons.

- **Speak your truth, even if you are worried about what your friends will think.** Lindsey was nervous about telling her friends that she was considering divinity school. She thought they'd all look at her like she had two heads, thinking she would one day become a crazy fundamentalist preacher. Turns out, the majority of people were curious to learn more about her decision, and very supportive of her interest in building a progressive spiritual community.
- **Focus more on the skills you want to build, and less on the career sector you are interested in.** Lindsey refused to let a specific career sector limit her potential. While she cultivated expertise for eight years in areas like climate change, political organizing, and start-up investment, she focused more on the skill she wanted to develop (building community). This allowed her to make the jump between two seemingly distinct lily pads: start-up investment and divinity school. I bet that the work she did cultivating meaningful relationships among investors and companies at New Media Ventures is going to serve her very well when she becomes a minister.
- **Don't go to grad school to please anyone else; go because you absolutely have to.** Trying to please your parents, or strangers you meet at dinner parties, is an exercise in futility. Had Lindsey listened to others, she probably would have pursued business school or a master's in public policy, which are far more "practical" degrees. Instead, she chose to listen to herself. As Lindsey astutely observed, "Grad school is a very expensive way to have an answer to the dreaded *What do you do?* question, or add an additional line on your résumé." Instead, think about the kinds of skills you want to hone, the network you want to build, and the general direction you want to go in your career. If grad school is essential to all those things, and you've exhausted other possibilities, then consider going.

When considering divinity school, Lindsey was told by one pastor, "Only go if you can't not go." That's as good advice as I've ever heard about whether to go to grad school.

Breakthrough Exercise: Is Graduate School Worth It?

If you're considering whether grad school is the right lily pad to leap to next, here are several questions you can ask yourself:

1. Will grad school provide me with a new skill set I need to learn or professional opportunities I don't already have that will help me get closer to my purpose?

2. Will grad school introduce me to a community of people who will inspire me and support me in reaching my potential? Can I *only* meet this community of people by attending grad school or is there another way to find this community?

3. Is now the right time for me to go to grad school? Do I have enough work/life experience to make what I'll learn valuable? (Recall that Conor lived abroad for a year and worked for over three years before realizing that law school would give him the skills he was lacking.)

4. Do I really want to go, or is another person in my life (parent, boss, coworker, friend) pressuring me to go to grad school?

5. What lifestyle sacrifices will I have to make in order to pay for grad school? Will having a lot of debt impact my ability to find meaningful work following grad school?

Kate's not the first person to go to grad school and realize that she wants to do something completely different with her life several years later. It's never too late to embrace the journey and leap lily pads, even if that means going from contract law to decorating homes at the age of thirty-two. Kate's breakthrough has already begun—she's been writing articles for a prestigious interior design magazine, and is planning on leaving her firm once she saves enough money. "I would advise people against going to law school as a catchall degree," says Kate. "Having a job that pays me a lot of money and is completely unsatisfying has made me realize that it's important to do the thing that you're good at and that you also happen to love. Of course I'm afraid that I won't succeed with my next move. But I'm also excited to finally know what I want to do next, and to truly believe in myself."

BREAKTHROUGH TAKEAWAYS

- There are people who have a clear intention behind why they are going to grad school and people who don't.
- Graduate school may offer an incredible opportunity to learn new skills, gain expertise, and build a network, which can increase your ability to make an impact in the areas you care about. However, it's important to ask yourself whether now is the right time for you to go back to school based on your purpose, and how having debt will affect your desired lifestyle and limit the choices you have once you graduate.

Don't go to grad school to please anyone else—go because you absolutely must for your purpose.

PART THREE

Build a Life That Matters

PART THREE

CHAPTER 9

What to Do When Someone Tells You You're Not Ready for Your Dreams

"Sometimes you have to play a long time to be able to play like yourself."
—MILES DAVIS

IT'S EASY TO give up when you're first getting started on a new path. A lot of people will give you advice, and it's hard to know whom to ignore and whom to listen to. My advice is to ignore anyone who tells you not to pursue your dreams, and listen to anyone who says you need to hustle harder.

It is never easy to quit your job; it is especially difficult when you truly believe in the mission of the organization you're working for, and even harder when you don't have another job or grad school lined up. Several years ago, when I told one colleague at the Peace Corps that I was leaving and moving to San Francisco, she replied, "Oh, wonderful, where are you going to be working?"

"I don't have a job yet," I replied.

"Oh, great, where are you going to graduate school?" she asked.

"I'm not going to grad school," I said.

"So you're going . . . *just for life*?" she wondered, dumbfounded. She looked at me like I was from another planet.

Just for life. As if life was not good enough.

In those first months after launching my writing career, few people besides my parents read my blog, and I spent more time trying to find part-time work than I did actually writing. I did some copywriting for a tech company and juggled part-time jobs for the Bold Academy and Hive, while briefly working as a host at a restaurant. I wasn't a very good host—instead of taking people's names for the wait list, I would space out and daydream, thinking of a blog post I was writing.

As I continued to blog, a few friends told me I should write a book. At first, I didn't even take them seriously. I thought they were joking. I laughed at them. But they weren't laughing back.

Thanks to these friends, I started to believe in myself. I began blogging more often and grew my following from one subscriber (my mom), to several friends, to a few thousand readers. Still, you'll recall that when I told one good friend I was writing a book, he said, "I'm pretty sure that book has already been written like a hundred times, by people a lot smarter than you. You're just wasting your time."

Remember: ignore people who tell you not to pursue your dreams. Sure, almost everything has been done before, but it hasn't been done by you yet, and that's all that matters. Did the IBM computer or the Nokia phone stop Steve Jobs? Did all those United airplanes with TV sets from 1975 and the world's most uncomfortable seats stop Richard Branson?

When I pitched my idea for a book about purpose-driven twentysome-things stuck in a quarter-life crisis, one editor told me, "It's an interesting idea, and you're a decent writer, but you're not qualified to get a book deal to write it. My advice is to self-publish so you practice writing and build your audience."

At this point, I had two options. One was to give up—the editor told me I wasn't qualified enough to get a book deal; maybe writing wasn't for me. My other option was to listen to her advice and hustle harder. I chose to listen to her feedback.

In July 2013, I ran a crowdfunding campaign so I could hire a professional editor and cover designer, and self-publish the book. Self-publishing offered an incredible opportunity to share my story and demonstrate the market potential of my work. As I discussed in the previous chapter, crowdfunding my book taught me the invaluable lesson that people will support you when you make the ask and when you start working with purpose. People I had never even met before gave me money for a book I hadn't even written yet—I didn't even have a table of contents, and people were paying for preorders!

A few months later, when I delivered the forty-five-thousand-word first draft to my editor, at least she was honest when she told me, "This is really depressing, I thought you were writing something people would be inspired to read." I gave the draft to a few of my campaign supporters, and they confirmed my editor's doubts.

I went back and read my first draft, and as my editor said, it needed work. I had written five thousand words on why society was evil—and an entire paragraph on why kids should stop drinking soda. I learned a lesson many young writers learn when they start writing: it's a lot easier to articulate what you're against than what you actually stand for.

At this point I could have quit, again. I could have taken my editor's doubts to mean I was an awful writer and had no business writing a book. Instead, I chose to listen to her feedback and work harder. After I made a commitment to my Passion Co. class, I locked myself in the library and spent six more months writing a new forty-five-thousand-word second draft. Every day, I'd bike over to the UCSF Library, walk up to the fourth floor, sit next to a window overlooking Golden Gate Park (on clear days you could see all the way to the Golden Gate Bridge and the Marin headlands), listen to Explosions in the Sky radio on Pandora, and write. The second draft was much stronger, and after eight drafts, my editor and I finally felt the book was ready to share with the world.

In 2014, my self-published version of *The Quarter-Life Breakthrough* became a best-seller and number one top-rated job-hunting book on Amazon.

I reached out to another editor friend and sent her a paperback copy of my book, along with a link to fifty five-star Amazon reviews of the book. Impressed with the progress I had made with self-publishing, the editor introduced me to her friend, an experienced literary agent in New York City. The agent was really excited about my positive message for twenty-somethings and signed me. It took about five months for us to finish a book proposal for a project based on my first book, an unconventional career guide for millennials seeking meaningful work.

The majority of the twenty-five different publishers we approached rejected our proposal, but a few showed interest, and in the summer of 2015 we agreed to a deal with TarcherPerigee to publish this book that you're reading right now.

The story of how it took me three years to get a book deal reminds us that rejection is part of the journey to meaningful work. You will get rejected. You will be told that you're not yet ready. Remember: This doesn't mean you should quit. Sometimes it means you must dig in and keep practicing.

Two years ago, when I told people at happy hour that I was self-publishing my first book, they raised their eyebrows and said, "Oh, you're *self-publishing*. So you're not actually a writer yet."

It hurt. But I used these comments as motivation to prove that I was serious about my work. After I secured a book deal, I noticed a few people started calling me a "real writer." They said, "Wow, you're writing a book for a New York City publisher, you're actually a *real writer* now!"

I think this sentiment is damaging to writers everywhere. You are a "real writer" the second you put pen to paper or start typing. You are a speaker the second you get in front of a room and speak. You are an artist the second you pick up a paintbrush. You are a businesswoman the second you sketch your idea on a napkin.

I don't think I got a book deal because I quit my job, took the leap, and followed my passion. I think I got a book deal because I embraced a new pursuit at the age of thirty and thought of myself as a "real writer" despite the fact that I was a beginner. I think I got a book deal because I kept blogging, even during those months when I wasn't making any money. I think I got a book deal because I kept going after being rejected the first time I tried to get published. I think I got a book deal because when my editor told me my first draft needed to be rewritten, I went back to the library and spent six more months writing. I think I got a book deal because instead of just writing a short query e-mail to secure an agent, I spent a year of my life writing a book—my book was my query letter.

I think I got a book deal because I hustled harder than I ever had in my life.

I'll be the first to resist the concept of "delayed gratification"—millennials want to make an impact, and we want to make it now. But the past three years have taught me that career fulfillment is not online dating. You can't just swipe right. Some things take more time, and a lot more effort.

If you want to have a meaningful career, you have to keep hustling for it.

Breakthrough Exercise: Embrace Rejection

Think of a recent experience at work where someone gave you honest feedback or rejected you. Maybe a supervisor told you to redo a project or that you weren't qualified for a promotion. How did you respond? Were you angry? Did you blame someone else? Did you quit?

Now consider how you could respond in a way that embraces rejection. Could you accept the feedback as a sign that you need to put in more time and effort? Could you accept that you need to work harder on a project, complete a second draft, or gain more experience before quitting? Think of two to three ways rejection could help you practice and keep going toward your goals.

BREAKTHROUGH TAKEAWAYS

- Ignore people who tell you not to pursue your dreams. Everything has been done before, but it hasn't been done by you yet, and that's all that matters.
- Rejection is part of the journey to meaningful work. Rejection doesn't mean you should quit. Sometimes it means you must dig in and keep practicing.

Career fulfillment takes time. If you want to find meaningful work, you have to be persistent.

CHAPTER 10

Get Your Breakthrough Hustle On

*"The most difficult thing is the decision to act,
the rest is merely tenacity."*
—AMELIA EARHART

THE ANTIDOTE TO fear is taking action toward our goals. But how do we take action when we know our goals are changing and that the journey to find meaningful work is not easy, quick, or simple? To put it bluntly: *we hustle*. We hustle harder than we've ever hustled before.

If me, my friends, or my father are any indication, most of us are going to be leaping lily pads to get closer to aligning our work with our purpose for a long time. It took me three years to make my writing a profitable endeavor. Three years is a long time. Recall the story of Ryan, who became a tech entrepreneur at the age of eleven when his uncle gave him his first Macintosh computer, and spent nearly twenty years as a tech entrepreneur before realizing that he was less interested in marketing software than empowering mission-driven leaders. Twenty years is a long time. This is a reminder that the journey calls for serious preparation: *breakthroughs require both personal hustle and outside help.*

In this chapter, you'll take action by getting your breakthrough hustle on. First, you'll write down the action items you know you need to do, and find accountability so you can make your breakthrough a reality. To prepare to share your gifts with others, you'll begin by taking care of yourself and designing your own self-love practice. Then, you'll plan your breakthrough and map out your breakthrough goals. In the following chapter, I'll share how I hustled for a year to start earning revenue from my public-speaking business. And in chapter 12, you'll build a support system of people who share your values and believe in your potential. All of the breakthrough hustlers featured in this book did not get where they are today alone. They got there because they found people to help them along the way.

WRITE IT DOWN

In Ted Gonder's "Smashing Fear" talk, there's a moment when he lets the audience know things are "about to get real." He asks everyone to stand up and take out their notebooks. This is *after* he shows YouTube videos of the honey badger sticking his head into a swarming beehive to extract the larvae, as well as Mike Tyson calmly taking endless jabs to the head only to use his impregnable defense to knock out his opponent with one perfectly timed, well-placed punch.

Ted asks everyone to rip out a sheet of paper and write down one thing they know they need to do that they've been scared of doing for months. "If you don't write something down," Ted says, "you won't do it." Then, each person exchanges papers with the person next to them, and promises to follow up in a week to make sure the other person has accomplished their task.

My one thing that I was scared to do was to start a blog and write my first blog post. I had been telling myself I was going to start a blog for two years, but I had never actually done it. When my accountability partner from Ted's exercise texted me the next weekend to see if I had started my blog, I remember thinking to myself, Crap, she remembered. I'm so screwed. I tried to think of excuses I could tell her that wouldn't make me look pathetic. *My girlfriend was in town visiting this weekend* (wait—I totally mentioned to her I didn't have a girlfriend). *My MacBook is broken* (no—that's ridiculous). *Work is crazy these days* (nope—I had mentioned to her I was bored out of my mind at work).

In the end, I realized it would probably be easier to write the darn blog post, rather than make up a stupid excuse. I went to WordPress, registered the domain name for my first blog (whatsupsmiley.com), and wrote my first blog post about how my best friend Andreas had officially deemed 2012

"The Year of Love." After putting it off for two years, the whole "starting a blog" thing cost me $18 and about twenty minutes of my time.

Looking back now, after writing more than a hundred blog posts and numerous pieces for other publications, and publishing two books, I can say that writing one sentence on a piece of paper and spending twenty minutes to create the blog changed my life.

Breakthrough Exercise: Ten Ten-Minute Action Items

Whenever I teach a class on finding meaningful work, I have one simple goal. I want participants to leave the workshop closer to their breakthrough than when they started. The way I achieve this goal is by telling participants to start small. I recommend making a list of all the action items you can do in the next thirty days to help you get closer to your purpose. Action items are not long-term undertakings like "quit my job," "move to India," "write a book," or "build a $3,000-a-month business." Action items are tasks that can be completed in ten minutes or less. Things like "buy a plane ticket to India," "open the Word doc for my new book," "buy the domain name for my website," "set up coffee with someone who works at a company I'm interested in."

Make a list of at least ten different ten-minute action items you can do in the next thirty days that will help you get closer to your breakthrough.

DO IT NOW

Have you ever known you needed to get something done, but been completely unable to do it? You procrastinate so hard that you do everything you could possibly do, except the one thing that actually needs to get done. When I first set out to write this book, it took me two weeks to even get started. During those two weeks, I did lots of things. I cleaned my room. I watered the plants. I did my laundry. I went to Target to buy a pack of gum. I bought a pack of gum, as well as a pair of sandals, and seven other things I didn't need. I organized my bookshelf by color. Unsatisfied, I then organized my bookshelf by genre. I collected all the pennies, nickels, and dimes in my room, and took them to the bank to redeem them for $13. Then I spent the $13 on an overpriced free-range chicken sandwich. I even called Comcast to ask them a question about my Internet bill, which took about forty-five minutes. If you ever catch yourself *calling Comcast* instead of getting your work done, you know you have reached the Procrastination Hall of Fame, and you have a problem.

During those two weeks, there was only one, very simple task that I needed to do to begin my book: open up a new Word document, click "Save As," type in "My New Book," and start typing a sentence. That's it. I probably could have done that in twenty-five seconds, but it took me two weeks. One way to keep yourself from procrastinating on your breakthrough is to complete the most intimidating task on your mind as quickly as possible. Something that you know you need to do, that you've been putting off forever, a task that will get you closer to your breakthrough.

When I was in high school, my cross-country coach would always tell us to place our running clothes on the floor next to our beds before we went to sleep. Why? To make it easier to roll out of bed at seven in the morning and go for a run in the freezing 20-degree Boston winter. Anything to make an intimidating task just a little bit easier.

So, what's your most intimidating task from your ten-minute action items? Maybe it's setting up a coffee date with a potential mentor. Maybe it's buying the domain name for your website. Maybe it's publishing a blog post that you've been scared to publish for weeks. Whatever that task is, you're going to do it now. By "now," I don't mean after you call Comcast. I mean *right now*.

FIND ACCOUNTABILITY

Finding an accountability buddy doesn't mean you have to join a cult-ish support group like Hair Club for Men. It just means you have to find one person to hold you accountable to your dreams. Remember my friend Evan, who asked me on the rooftop bar of the Hotel Shangri-La in Santa Monica,

"Why would you be doing anything less than maximizing your full potential in life?" After that conversation, I told Evan I was going to quit my job.

Usually, when you tell someone you're going to quit your job, they're like, *"Yeah, dude, you said that six months ago. You're never gonna do it. See you next Friday for beers."*

Not when you have an accountability buddy. When I told Evan I was going to quit my job, he asked me one simple question. "When? When are you going to have the talk with your boss?"

Evan texted me every single week after our rooftop conversation, "Smiley, have you had the talk with your boss yet?" I'd be in meetings with high-level officials at the White House, getting texts and phone calls from Evan, "Smiley, have you had the talk with your boss yet?" The dude started calling me so often I thought the Secret Service was going to arrest me. "Smiley, have you had the talk with your boss yet?"

But you know what? The only reason I did eventually have the talk with my boss, the only reason I did quit my job, the only reason I did move across the country to San Francisco, the only reason I started writing, and the only reason you're reading this book right now, is because people like Evan held me accountable. When you find believers, you find accountability, and when you find accountability your dreams come true.

Breakthrough Exercise: Accountability Buddy

Pick someone you trust that you don't know very well. I've found the best accountability buddies are *not* your best friend, partner, or boss. People that know you too well have a tendency to let you off the hook too easily. Find someone you just met at a party or a friend of a friend. If you're reading this book on an airplane, it could even just be the person sitting next to you. Exchange phone numbers with this person, then ask them to hold you accountable to one of your Ten-Minute Action Items by texting you in twenty-four hours to make sure you've completed your task. Ask them what they want to be held accountable for, and remember to text your accountability buddy in twenty-four hours to make sure they've accomplished their task.

GO OUTSIDE YOUR COMFORT ZONE

There's an episode of the popular HBO series *Girls* where Hannah—an unemployed freelance writer living with her best friends in Brooklyn—goes to a job interview at a magazine and asks the editor what she should write about. The editor tells her she should have a threesome and then write about it. Hannah looks at her like she's crazy, explains that she can't have a threesome because she has enough trouble as it is figuring out where to put her attention on *one* person's body. The editor then shows Hannah a framed image of her comfort zone and an arrow pointing to a circle outside the comfort zone, with the words *where the magic happens*.

Breakthroughs involve change, and many of those changes will probably be outside your comfort zone. Your breakthrough is about experimentation and trying new things to get you closer to your goals. Deepa Subramaniam did just that, with incredible rewards.

Deepa, now thirty-four years old, had been working at Adobe for ten years, ever since she graduated from college. Deepa is very talented, and she steadily worked her way up to becoming a principal product manager, meaning she managed a team of product managers, engineers, and designers to take strategic ideas from conception to execution, quickly and correctly.

During her tenth year at the company, she began to get restless and eager for a career change. "I am not a huge risk taker. I tend to treat change the way a shy boy might ask out a girl—sniffing around and working up courage before deciding to take action," explains Deepa. "Having hit this huge milestone, a decade at a large and established company, I thought back to what I envisioned for myself when I was in high school and college. I had always seen myself working as a leader within an organization focused on making the world a better place. Though Adobe's mission to empower the creative class with the best tools and services was something I felt passionate about, I was starting to realize that this mission wasn't in total alignment with what I wanted to spend my time and energy doing as I got older."

In order to figure out what her purpose was, Deepa went outside her comfort zone and started making some new friends. "I started talking to more people, younger and older, about what they were doing, how they were doing it, what organizations piqued their interest, and so on," she says. "I expanded my social circle outside of my usual 'tech-y' friends, and made a special effort to talk to people of varied backgrounds. This was how I stumbled into the social impact space where many organizations, both nonprofit and for-profit, sounded like they could use my particular skills and strengths. The 'light' went off when I realized I was spending more time reading blogs and articles about technology used at the intersection of social change, instead of the web design- and web development-focused materials I would normally consume throughout my day."

Around the time she was branching out and trying to learn more about the social impact space, she saw a tweet from charity: water, a nonprofit organization bringing clean, safe drinking water to people in developing nations. The tweet caught her eye and landed her on charity: water's "We're Hiring" page, where she noticed an open position for their director of product. Within minutes of reading it, she knew she was the right fit for the job.

"The posting called specifically for someone with my exact skill set and desires," says Deepa. "This job was in the space I wanted to be in, and would be leveraging all of the things I naturally liked to do, and did well."

By reaching out to friends, Deepa found a former charity: water employee, who introduced her to the founder. After she told the founder she was interested in the position, she went outside of her comfort zone even further and got her breakthrough hustle on.

She knew Adobe had a program that provided paid sabbaticals to employees after five years with the company, so she pitched Adobe on letting her use her six-week sabbatical to volunteer for charity: water. Adobe agreed, and Deepa used the time as a way to try out living in New York and working for charity: water. Instead of quitting her job at Adobe, moving to New York and hoping for the best, she used one of our meaningful job-search techniques: *she tested an opportunity through a short-term apprenticeship.*

A few weeks into her trial, Deepa discovered she loved working for the nonprofit, and that she also loved living in New York. She decided to leave her job at Adobe, and took a significant pay cut to work as charity: water's director of product. While Deepa was initially hesitant to leave a lucrative job at a company she had been working at for ten years (and who wouldn't be?), she made her transition by *taking tangible, incremental steps* toward her next lily pad. First, she started hanging out with people other than her "tech-y" friends. Then, she researched more about the social impact space, using blogs and Twitter to learn about new opportunities.

Then, she used her friend networks to get in touch with the staff at charity: water. Instead of immediately quitting her job and moving to New York on a whim, she tested the new job and new city out with a six-week apprenticeship. After ten years going down one career path, Deepa successfully found a new way of using her skills to make an impact—all because she went outside her comfort zone.

Was charity: water Deepa's last lily pad? What do you think? Nearly two years after starting at charity: water, Deepa went outside her comfort zone (again). She took the skills she had gained over twelve years working in tech as a product manager at Adobe and as head of product for a clean water nonprofit, and applied for a position as director of product for Hillary Clinton's 2016 presidential campaign. Deepa got the job, and she's now figuring out how to use technology to mobilize supporters, raise money, and build digital tools to help the campaign be more successful.

"I have always looked up to Hillary since I was a little girl," Deepa told me. "My family has been Clinton supporters for a long time. When this once-in-a-lifetime opportunity presented itself, I just went for it. I think I had grown more comfortable saying yes from my experience leaving Adobe. I had flexed my 'playing with fear' muscle."

When you start getting comfortable going outside your comfort zone and trying new things, anything is possible. When you build up the skills you need to distinguish yourself from the crowd, you can reach your potential.

With a traditional career ladder mind-set, Deepa would have never gone from working in software, to a clean water nonprofit, to a political campaign, in the span of less than three years. But, as we know, careers do not move up and down in straight lines. Rather than be married to a sector (like nonprofit/for-profit, or software/politics), Deepa was married to a skill. "Technology is my medium; it's what I love," explains Deepa. "Using technology to solve hard problems. Whether that's applied to the for-profit space like I did at Adobe, the water and sanitation space like I did at charity: water, or the political arena like at Hillary for America, it's that application I find interesting. I feel like I'm learning hundreds of things every single day, because it's always a new application."

It's the application of how to use technology to solve something important that gets Deepa excited. When you find a medium or a skill that you can test in new environments, it ensures you become a lifelong learner. There is no shortage of companies and situations that need technological innovation, so my guess is that Deepa will have a fulfilling career for many years to come.

PRACTICE SELF-LOVE

Like many eighteen- to thirty-four-year-olds who have moved back in with their parents after living on their own, I've done it twice. One time was a few months after graduating from college when I was figuring things out, and another time was when I was twenty-seven and unemployed. Moving back home with your parents has a bad rap. I think of *Seinfeld*'s George Costanza going around New York City, trying to get a date by saying, "I'm unemployed, and I live with my parents."

But it certainly has its perks: saving money on rent, a refrigerator full of food, and getting to spend time with people who love and support you. On the flip side, there's constant pressure to answer the inevitable question: *So, what the hell are you doing with your life?* (Or *When are you getting out of here, and have you thought about law school?*)

In my experience, it's easy to get overwhelmed when you move back home, experience fear of failure, and get stuck (especially when you're unemployed). When I was living at home at the age of twenty-seven, I was applying to jobs unsuccessfully and feeling like I'd never in a million years have a breakthrough. One night, I went out with a friend who asked me a powerful question: "What do you do every day to take care of yourself?" When I didn't say anything, she pressed me. "How do you practice self-love every day?"

Now, maybe it's because I grew up in Boston, where it's 22 degrees all winter long, and a good number of people spend much of their adult lives driving around like madmen and cursing out pedestrians, but *self-love* was not something I was familiar with. When I was living in DC, overworked and stressed, I *definitely* wasn't taking care of myself—and I got shingles! I didn't give myself time to eat well, see friends, meditate, write in my journal, or exercise. If you don't take care of yourself, it is nearly impossible to reach your goals or help anyone else reach theirs.

Starting to hustle doesn't translate to finding job postings online and applying to as many as you can. Starting to hustle means you spend time doing things you love, with the people you love. It also means learning how to be kind to yourself. As my friend Amber Rae, an artist, writer, and entrepreneur, reminds me, "When we optimize for our health and wellness, we can fully share our gifts with the world." She often asks, *What do you need on a daily basis to feel like the best version of yourself?*

START DATING YOURSELF

It seems that every other conversation I have is with people my age freaking out about being single. *Smiley, what am I gonna do, get on Tinder, is that all I have left? Smiley, how am I supposed to meet someone when everyone attractive and dateable is already taken? Smiley, I can't go to another wedding without a plus one, it's embarrassing! Smiley, I want to have a family and I'm thirty and single—my life is worthless!*

These conversations often surprise me. First off, if so many amazing people are single, why is everyone having so much trouble meeting the right partner? I now keep a running tab in my Moleskine journal of cool people I know who are single, and I cross-reference the list once every two weeks for potential matches—I'm like a boutique Hinge.

Second, and more alarming, is why people are so distraught about being single. I spent the better part of my late twenties (all right, my late twenties and my early thirties) single, and while I could make up a horror story about how miserable I was, the truth is I've never been happier. Rather than stress about how hard it was to meet the perfect woman at the age of thirty (and whether it was appropriate to wear running shoes on dates), I decided to forget about dating altogether.

Instead, I decided to start dating myself.

When you start dating yourself, your mind-set shifts. Rather than define your own self-worth based on whether someone else swipes right at your photo or whether someone else wants to go home with you, you determine your own self-worth based on how you're spending your time. You can commit to personal projects, set aside time for self-reflection and self-care, and discover new career aspirations. Instead of simply going through the motions, you're in the driver's seat of your own life.

If you're struggling with online dating or stressing about being the only single person at your friend's wedding (don't worry, that happened to me three times last summer!), my recommendation is to spend a few weeks dating yourself.

1. **Treat yourself.** Take yourself out on your perfect date. Go out to your favorite restaurant, order exactly what you want to eat, and drink a glass of red wine. Buy yourself a new shirt or pair of shoes. Go to the bookstore and buy a new book you're dying to read. Take yourself to a show this weekend—music, theater, comedy—whatever you love most. Go to a movie by yourself and sit in the exact seat you want to sit in. Stay up late and watch episodes of your favorite show on Netflix. Go on an adventure to a place you've never been before.
2. **Take care of yourself.** Go for a run. Take a long urban hike. Go to a yoga class you never have time to go to. Meditate. Take a nap in the sun. Take a nap in the shade. Take a bath. Get a massage. Cook your favorite meal. Order delivery and eat it in bed. Wake up early and read a book that has been sitting on your shelf for months. Taking care of yourself may mean doing nothing, which can actually be quite productive. Every weekend, my friend Evan Kleinman blocks off several hours in his calendar as "time for doing nothing." During that time, when people text him to hang out, he responds, "Sorry dude, I'm busy. I'm busy doing nothing."
3. **Create yourself.** Write in your journal. Write a blog post. Write a short story. Write a book (disclaimer: I did this and as a result was single for nearly three years, so plan accordingly). Take a letterpress class. Paint. Draw. Take photos. Make a short film. Learn to code. Learn a new language. Design your new website. Come up with a business idea.
4. **Engage yourself.** Find a friend working on a project that interests you and see how you can get involved. Volunteer in your community. Push yourself outside your comfort zone by going solo to an event that sounds fun. Start a group meet-up for an activity you love, like acroyoga, cooking, poetry, or graphic design.

See, being single isn't so bad. If you're in a serious relationship, and jealous of all the fun us single people are having because we're dating ourselves, you *should* be jealous. You're missing out! You can date yourself, too, even if you're engaged or married—it's not cheating to date yourself!

Don't worry, it's not permanent. I want someone to come home and snuggle with, just like most people. I want to have a family someday. I'm not telling you to stop dating or abandon your lifelong goal of being an amazing parent. I'm just saying that dating yourself for a few weeks might help you discover who you are and what you want. It might help you stop worrying about what other people think of your sixth Tinder photo (or stress about whether you should even *have* a sixth Tinder photo—who the hell has six Tinder photos?!) and start thinking about how you want to spend your days. It might inspire you to explore a new passion or find a new job. It might give you the time to launch the project or embark on the adventure you've always dreamed of.

If you're lucky, dating yourself might even bring you closer to the partner you've been searching for.

Breakthrough Exercise: Self-Love Rituals

Whether you are single or madly in love (or madly in love with someone who is not madly in love with you), what are three things you can do to start dating yourself this week? Think about ways you can **treat yourself**, **take care of yourself**, **create yourself**, and **engage yourself**. If you're stuck, think about ways you can *do nothing* this weekend. Each week, pick one new self-love ritual to incorporate into your weekly routine. Note: these self-love rituals may become part of your desired lifestyle requirements. Consider whether a job that doesn't allow you to pursue these rituals on a regular basis is the right fit for you.

MAKE A VISION BOARD

One evening in Washington, DC, before I left my job, I came home from a long day at work to find three of my roommates sitting around our dining room table. Katie, Elisabet, and Leslie had laid out a huge pile of (mostly women's lifestyle) magazines, scissors, glue sticks, and colored construction paper.

"Smiley, join us," they said. "We're making vision boards!" In my typical, cynical manner, I laughed at them. "I'm not cutting pictures out of a magazine—what is this, fourth grade? I'm too busy for this Oprah-induced foolishness. I'm gonna check my work BlackBerry for the fifty-eighth time today."

They proceeded to make vision boards without me. Even my other roommate made a vision board, although his consisted of only a koala bear, a rotisserie chicken, and a giant bottle of beer. I felt kind of left out, so I sat down and awkwardly started looking through the magazines, anxious, not choosing anything to cut out. After five minutes, I got distracted and gave up. But my roommates pestered me for a week about not making a vision board. Finally, I sat down, alone, deep in serious thought, and perused the pages of *Cosmopolitan*.

My vision board for my breakthrough, which I still keep taped to my door, featured pictures of places I wanted to travel and spend time (Barcelona, the woods, the beach, San Francisco), things I wanted to eat and drink (avocado, coffee, popsicles, bowls of pho), activities I wanted to do a lot of (write, read, run, sun salutations), and things I wanted to experience (risk, freedom, change, growth, relaxation), and some random stuff (Michael Jackson dancing). Yes, I also cut out a picture from *Glamour* of two people kissing.

It was difficult for me, as I imagine it is for most men, to be vulnerable with my emotions. It was difficult for me to take myself seriously. That was the first time I had ever made a vision board, and nearly every single vision on my board came true. Using scissors and a glue stick has a strange way of taking you back to when you were a kid, when creating and dreaming were second nature. Feminist Gloria Steinem once said, "Without leaps of imagination, or dreaming, we lose the excitement of possibilities. Dreaming, after all, is a form of planning." Having a breakthrough is beginning to dream again.

Breakthrough Exercise: Vision Boarding

What are your visions for your breakthrough? Make a vision board by cutting out pictures and words from old magazines. Think of **activities** you want to do a lot of this year, **places** where you want to spend time, and **emotions** you want to feel.

MAP OUT YOUR BREAKTHROUGH GOALS

When I set a date to leave my job, I was stressing about what I was going to do for money after my last day at work, how I was going to find an affordable apartment in San Francisco, and how I was going to find a job when I got there. In order to keep myself from freaking out every night before bed, I mapped out my one-month and six-month goals in my journal.

Massive goals can be overwhelming, but when you write your goals down, achieving them becomes possible. Appreciate the value of each baby step. Check out my Breakthrough Goal Map for reference, and feel free to come back and complete your Breakthrough Goal Map once you've finished reading this book. You can also download the Breakthrough Goal Map at smileyposwolsky.com.

My Quarter-Life Breakthrough Goal Map

Name: _____

Date: _____

My personal definition of meaningful work

MEANINGFUL WORK
reflects who you are:
reflects what your interests are:
allows you to share your gifts to help others:
provides a community of believers that will support your dreams:
is financially viable given your desired lifestyle:

My purpose, right now, is to find a job or opportunity that

My most intimidating task, which I'll do right now

My ten ten-minute action items

My one-month goal

My six-month goal

My accountability buddy

Five people for my Breakthrough Advisory Board

Three supportive communities I'll join

Three asks I'll make to my community

My weekly self-love rituals

Three investments I'll make in my breakthrough

Smiley's Quarter-Life Breakthrough Goal Map

My personal definition of meaningful work

MEANINGFUL WORK:

reflects who you are: Smiley, positive, inspiring, funny, creative

reflects what your interests are: writing, speaking, social entrepreneurship, millennials

allows you to share your gifts to help others: writing, speaking, positivity, meaningful work

provides a community of believers that will support your dreams: SF, entrepreneurs, social change makers

is financially viable given your desired lifestyle: make enough $ to pay rent in SF, pay off student loans, work-life balance, ample time for running and yoga, time for my sister and friends, eat well, and enjoy the Bay Area

My purpose, right now, is to find a job or opportunity that

allows me to share my gifts for writing, speaking, and inspiring millennials to find meaningful work and go after their dreams, and support myself while living with fun and creative people in San Francisco.

My most intimidating task, which I'll do right now

Start my blog!

My most ten-minute action items

1. Schedule meeting with my boss to have "the talk"
2. Schedule coffee dates with coworkers to see if they have contacts in SF
3. Buy domain name for my blog
4. Write first blog post
5. Schedule DC good-bye party
6. Buy one-way plane ticket to SF
7. Buy + read *The Artist's Way* by Julia Cameron
8. Buy + read *The War of Art* by Steven Pressfield
9. Research job opportunities in SF
10. E-mail StartingBloc contacts and writing contacts

My one-month goal

- Explain my plan to my boss (and my parents), thank my colleagues at Peace Corps for an amazing experience
- Limit expenses, start saving money for my move

My six-month goal

- Move from DC, be living in SF, pursuing writing and supporting social entrepreneurs
- Find an affordable place in SF (God help me)
- Find a new job in SF and make some money

My accountability buddy

- Evan Walden

Five people for my Breakthrough Advisory Board

1. My sister
2. Nathaniel Koloc
3. Ted Gonder
4. Sydney Malawer
5. Ryan Goldberg

Three supportive communities I'll join

1. StartingBloc
2. Passion Co.
3. Camp Grounded

Three asks I'll make to my community

1. Job contacts in writing
2. Connections to writers and social entrepreneurs in SF
3. Connections to people in the leadership + personal development space in SF

My weekly self-love rituals

Treat myself: Rewatch Season 4 of *The Wire*, read *The New Yorker*, go to the farmers' market

Take care of myself: Run 3x/week, yoga 1x/week, start meditating, eat lots of pho

Create myself: Daily journaling, weekly blog posts, design my blog

Engage myself: Volunteer at food festival, support friend's Kickstarter campaign, go to two meet-ups

Three investments I'll make in my breakthrough

1. Attend StartingBloc Institute
2. Attend Passion Co. program
3. Volunteer at Bold Academy

BREAKTHROUGH TAKEAWAYS

- The antidote to fear is taking action toward our goals.
- The journey to leap between lily pads and find your next opportunity will never be quick or easy. There is no magic bullet. That's why successful breakthroughs require both personal hustle and outside help.

First, write down the action items you know you need to do, and find someone to hold you accountable to your goals. Second, start planning for your breakthrough now: practice self-love by dating yourself, make a vision board, and map out your breakthrough goals.

CHAPTER 11

Persistence Trumps Passion:
Lessons in Breakthrough Hustling

"The reason a lot of people do not recognize opportunity is because it usually goes around wearing overalls looking like hard work."
—THOMAS A. EDISON

I HAVE BEEN a professional public speaker for a little over a year. It took dozens of speaking engagements and months of hustling to finally get my first paid gig, but I recently signed with CAMPUSPEAK, an agency that books motivational speakers on college campuses across the country, and spoke at a corporate conference, where I made more money in twenty minutes than I had in months.

Ten thousand dollars—for less than half an hour's work—is a sweet payday. To have the opportunity to travel around the country and speak to twentysomethings about how to work with purpose is a dream, but it's a dream that took a lot more than twenty minutes to achieve. Breakthrough hustling is a lot like learning to ride a bike. The hardest part is starting, but once you get going, you become a pro. This chapter offers a few practical lessons in breakthrough hustling I learned on the path to becoming a professional public speaker that can help anyone get started on achieving their breakthrough.

LESSON 1: INNER AUTHORITY IS MORE IMPORTANT THAN CAREER LADDER AUTHORITY

A friend recently asked me, "Smiley, what gives you the authority to go onstage and tell people what to do with their careers?"

I answered his question honestly. "Nothing. Nothing *gives me* the authority to go onstage and speak. I just started doing it. I gave myself the authority."

There are two kinds of authority in life. The first is external and the second is internal, and most people are far too preoccupied with building up their external *career ladder authority*. Career ladder authority is what our formal education prepares us for. School, standardized tests, college, getting a master's degree, getting published, getting a job with a reputable company, making a comfortable salary, receiving a prestigious award—all of the signposts we put on our résumé or LinkedIn, all of the things that impress employers, our parents, our friends on Facebook, our colleagues at happy hour. We spend most of our lives worrying about our self-worth as defined by society's currency.

Inner authority is not defined by society; it is defined by you. Nothing gives me the authority to get onstage and talk. No one *told me* to do that. No one gave me permission to do that. No one ever told me I was an "author" or a "speaker." One day, I just decided to write a book. Then, I just started speaking about it. It's that simple (and impossible). From a young age, we're told to wait for *society* to give us the green light, but that green light doesn't really exist. It doesn't matter where you went to school or how little experience you have. If you cultivate your *inner authority*, you will step into your greatness. Inner authority is the power that drives authors to write books, entrepreneurs to take huge risks, and leaders to change the world.

LESSON 2: CALL YOURSELF WHAT YOU WANT TO BE

If you are not confident enough to put the words "public speaker" on your website or your business card, you can be certain people won't pay you to speak to them. If you are not confident enough to call yourself a writer, no one is going to pay you to write for them. No one is ever going to pay you for something that you don't have the confidence to charge for. If you want to be a public speaker, call yourself a public speaker. A "real public speaker." Tell your mom you are a public speaker. Tell your friends you are a public speaker. Tell your past clients you are a public speaker. Sharing your gifts with the world will help you attract new clients and opportunities. Put yourself out there and call yourself what you are.

LESSON 3: START TODAY

The first time I spoke about my self-published book was at Alley Cat Books, a cozy independent bookstore in the Mission District of San Francisco. I rented out the gallery space for $100 and invited thirty friends to hear my story, eat cheese and crackers from Trader Joe's, and drink PBRs.

I put together my own book tour, which included unpaid speaking gigs on my friend's front porch in Washington, DC, at a sports bar in Philly, an auto body shop turned beer garden on Atlantic Avenue in Brooklyn, and from the bema inside my parent's synagogue in Boston. A childhood friend joked that the last time he had been to Temple was for my Bar Mitzvah, in 1996 (when I also spoke from the bema and everyone threw candy at me).

I decided to speak anywhere and everywhere about the book. I'd bust out my intro line, "Raise your hand if you've ever had a quarter-life crisis!" on the BART in San Francisco, the Metro in DC, the subway in New York, the T in Boston, and the Underground in London. I even tried to give my spiel about the book on the Bolt Bus on the road in between DC and New York.

The lesson here is that you don't need to wait for an invitation from TED or South by Southwest to be a public speaker, you don't need an invitation from Richard Branson or Marc Andreessen to be an entrepreneur, and you don't need an invitation from Random House or Simon & Schuster to be an author.

You simply must start. If you want to be a public speaker, get a room full of people together and speak your truth. The room can be a bar, your local coffee shop, or your friend's office. Create an Eventbrite page for your event, e-mail your friends, and share your event on Facebook and Twitter. It's impossible to get good at something without practicing first. Taking the first step will help build your audience, develop client relationships, and get future paid engagements.

LESSON 4: PRACTICE FOR AT LEAST SIX MONTHS

Anyone passionate about public speaking has probably spent hours (if not days) at their desk watching their favorite TED talks over and over again, thinking to themselves, One day that will be me, one day that will be me.

Why not make today that day? Start storyboarding, writing, and practicing your very own TED talk right now. A TED talk is basically just a fifteen-minute talk that tells a personal story or lesson learned, and takes the audience on an engaging journey. You don't need to be famous to tell a fifteen-minute personal story, and you don't need an invitation from TED to tell your story, either.

When I first got excited about public speaking, I went over to my friend Satya's house since Satya has a really large whiteboard wall. I outlined my whole talk on the whiteboard and asked myself these key questions: What is the single most important point of my talk? What are three examples I can give to support my message? Who is my target audience? What is the feeling I want my audience to have after my talk?

Once I had the basics outlined, I wrote up my notes and started practicing by myself in the park near my house. A lot of people talk to themselves in San Francisco, so no one seemed to mind. Once you feel ready, you can either put together your own event or apply to speak at an event near you. There are plenty of communities that open their doors to energetic new speakers. Check out Toastmasters, Ignite, and Meetup.com. There are also thousands of independently organized TEDx events in cities around the world, and you can apply directly via their website. It often helps to have a personal connection with an event organizer, so if you don't have one, use your network or social media to find someone who does.

When I actually delivered my talk at TEDxYouth@Mile High in Denver, Colorado, in front of two thousand high school students, over six months had gone by since I first outlined it on Satya's whiteboard. Six months is a long time, but the only reason I ever even gave a TED talk was because one day I started outlining it at my friend's house. Then I practiced it every single week for six months. You have to start somewhere, so why not right here, right now?

Breakthrough Exercise: Practice Your TED Talk

Whether you are a professional speaker, entrepreneur, intrapreneur, or introvert, public speaking is a necessary life skill. Knowing what matters most to you (and being able to share your ideas with others) is essential for a breakthrough. People who build a meaningful career know their own story. They know their *why*. When you know your *why*, it's easier to know *where* you're headed.

So, if you were to give a fifteen-minute TED talk to a room full of strangers, what would it be about? *What are the life-defining moments you identified in chapter 1? What social issues do you care most about? What injustice infuriates you? What is your why?*

Now, think about the delivery of your story: *How can you share your unique life experiences with the audience in a way that is entertaining, funny, or moving? What will the audience be moved to do once your talk is over?*

LESSON 5: ALWAYS GET MARKETING ASSETS

A year ago, I was attending a conference where my friend and speaking mentor Antonio Neves, an award-winning broadcast journalist and college leadership speaker who has been a professional speaker for five years, was delivering a keynote. Antonio handed his iPhone to me right before his excellent talk on "How to Be Less Awkward," and said, "Take a few pics for me." I just assumed the conference would have a professional photographer that would take way better photos than my phone. Turns out, I was wrong. Good thing I took a few pics, or he wouldn't have had anything to post on social media.

Always ensure that you get marketing assets like photos or videos at your events. After any project you work on, it's important to reach out to the event organizer and get a testimonial by asking, *Would you recommend my work to a friend?* Testimonials provide social proof that you can use on your website to get future work. One other thing: create an e-mail mailing list and always get e-mail addresses of people who show up to your events. Even if only five people show up to an event you've been planning for months, that's five people who might become future clients. My strategy is to pass around a sign-up sheet for my mailing list toward the end of my talk. Anyone who signs up gets a helpful quarter-life breakthrough resources guide.

LESSON 6: PARTNER WITH MISSION-ALIGNED BRANDS AND ORGANIZATIONS

As a speaker or entrepreneur, you often find yourself standing in front of a room, but trust me, you won't get in front of a room unless you collaborate with other partners. One of the most useful strategies I've incorporated into my speaking business is to partner with mission-aligned brands. One of my favorite places to speak is General Assembly. General Assembly (GA) is an innovative vocational school for adults, with locations all around the world. They offer coding, product management, experience design, and other technology-related courses, like the immersive course Yoni Binstock took in front-end development.

Why would someone like me, who talks about building a meaningful career, want to speak at a tech school? Because GA and I share the same audience. Most GA students are young professionals in their twenties or thirties who are making career changes and trying to get their technology and business skills up to par so they can land a new job. Their students are hustlers—they are all willing to invest in their career capital to find meaningful work—that's why they are going to events at GA. They are the perfect candidates to put my words into action. Whenever I do an event at GA in San Francisco or Los Angeles, I know I'm going to be speaking in front of a room full of fifty or more people who want to be there and who share similar values.

The best reason to find a mission-aligned partner? Comarketing opportunities. Whenever I do an event at GA, they blast their e-mail list of thousands of subscribers with info about my event. These are people I would never be able to reach, who can now click on a link and learn more about my work. All of the people on my e-mail list also get to learn about other classes and events happening at GA; it's a win-win. Make a list of the leading companies working in your area of expertise and see if you can build a mission-aligned partnership.

LESSON 7: SUCCESS IS CHANGING ONE PERSON'S LIFE, NOT HAVING THOUSANDS OF TWITTER FOLLOWERS

For one of my first corporate gigs, I got booked to speak to junior analysts at Deloitte's New York City office. I can't tell you how excited I was to speak at one of the most prestigious consulting firms in the world. I got my suit dry-cleaned for the gig, and I couldn't sleep the night before because I was so nervous. When I arrived at the plush lobby of Deloitte's New York City office, only four people had shown up to listen to me. A few others stopped by but left after thirty seconds, staying just long enough to grab a slice of the free pizza Deloitte provided.

My friend who works at Deloitte, who helped organize the gig, had given me only one instruction: "Smiley, you can say whatever you want, just don't explicitly tell my employees to quit their jobs." I told my personal story to those four people, sold one copy of my book, and left the gig feeling like the trip to New York wasn't even worth it.

One year later, I was emceeing the Hive Global Leaders Program, and a woman came up to me and said, "Hey, Smiley, I know you!" She was one of the four people who came to my talk at Deloitte. Turns out the talk had given her the confidence to make the transition from being an unhappy management consultant working eighty hours a week on projects she didn't care about, to more fulfilling work in impact investing. (To my friend who works at Deloitte: I swear I didn't tell her to quit her job, I just told her to listen to her heart. If you want me to come speak at Deloitte again, I'm down!)

If you want to make an impact, all you need is one person. If one person shows up, that's one person who has taken time out of their busy day to come to your event. That's one life you can change.

You don't need to have a huge platform or a huge audience to be relevant. You just need to be able to inspire one person. No one cares how many Twitter followers you have. The only thing that matters is whether you can empower your audience. You never know who's in the room, and you never know whose life you're going to touch. Always show up and perform as if the president were sitting in the front row.

LESSON 8: CELEBRATE SMALL WINS

A few months ago, I was complaining to a friend about how crappy my e-mail newsletter was, and how I needed to redo my website. "Smiley, shut up," he said. "You just got paid to speak about your book. That's freakin' awesome. Sure, you have more work to do and things could be better—things could always be better—but you should acknowledge yourself for that accomplishment."

You know what I did? I shut up. I thought to myself, Wow, I just got paid to speak about my book. About *my* book. That *is* freakin' awesome!

Don't forget to acknowledge yourself for the small wins, the things you're doing right now that are influencing others. Did you write a blog post recently? Did you speak at an event? Did you coordinate an event? Were you featured in a website or publication? Did you shoot a new video? Did you launch a crowdfunding campaign? Did you teach a class or facilitate a workshop? Did you finish an important project at work?

Take a moment to congratulate yourself. Cherish each creative accomplishment you make. This moment matters more than what you *could* be doing or *should* be doing or what *others* are doing. You can never go back and feel what it was like to be in this moment, so before you rush on to the next milestone, acknowledge yourself for doing what you're doing right now.

LESSON 9: STAY HUMBLE

When I was preparing to deliver my TEDx talk in front of two thousand high school students in Denver, I was nervous that the audience wouldn't relate to the themes of my talk because they were too young. Some people gave me the (bad) advice that I should dumb down my talk to make it more applicable to teenagers. I didn't listen to them, and I'm glad I didn't. Turns out high school students also face Facebook-induced FOMO and are nervous about making the right career choices, just like twentysomethings. Never ever assume that your audience is "too young" (or "too old") or too anything. Never assume that your audience doesn't understand what you are talking about. Many of the high school students I met in Denver were as brilliant, ambitious, and purpose-driven as people who are twice their age.

Chances are your audience knows more than you think, and they might even know more than you. Never speak down to your audience. Instead, engage them, ask them for feedback, and treat them like equals.

LESSON 10: GIVE YOURSELF PRESS

As cool as it would be for *The New York Times* to cover my next speaking engagement, unless I change my name to Aziz Ansari, it's probably not going to happen. But that doesn't mean getting press coverage for your work is impossible. A great strategy is to make a list of the most relevant blogs and online publications in your niche. If you work in nutrition, identify the top nutrition websites and the health and wellness blogs you read.

Even though many of these blogs and publications have fancy websites, they are likely in desperate need of good content. Provide them with an engaging guest blog post that demonstrates your expertise in your niche. Although some publications often don't pay for content, you never know who is reading. I'm hesitant to tell you to write for free, but I certainly did it a lot over the past three years when I was launching my writing and speaking career. I wrote a piece for *Fast Company*, about how millennial entrepreneurs are seeking meaningful work, which led to the corporate gig where I got paid $10,000 for a twenty-minute talk. I never got paid for writing the piece (it probably would have only been a $150 check anyway, which barely even makes it worth it, considering the piece took me two weeks to write), but the piece clearly was worth my time in the long run.

LESSON 11: PERSISTENCE TRUMPS PASSION

While I keep mentioning that I got paid $10,000 for a twenty-minute talk, which is true, I fail to mention that it took me nearly two years to make that happen. Someone who read my *Fast Company* article about millennial entrepreneurs reached out to me about speaking at a large corporate conference in the spring of 2014. While the conference paid my travel and lodging expenses, it didn't compensate me for speaking on a panel about millennial entrepreneurship. One year later, however, colleagues I met at that conference booked me for the $10,000 gig. Patience matters. Hustle matters. It takes time to build relationships with your clients, and it takes time to hone your craft.

It's easy to post an inspirational quote on Facebook. *Follow your passion and live the dream!* What we really should be posting is, *Hustle as hard as you can, and when you get rejected, don't stop, keep hustling even harder.* It's not easy to do the work. It's not easy to practice for an entire year.

Living the dream isn't chilling on a beach, it's doing everything possible to make your unique contribution to the world. Living the dream is dedication to a higher purpose. I don't think I made $10,000 in twenty minutes because I followed my passion to be a public speaker. I think I got the $10,000 gig because I found the persistence to commit to a long-term goal. The breakthrough hustlers I look up to always are trying to get better; they are always willing to practice, even if it means taking a risk and being uncomfortable sometimes. They know that practice and persistence matter more than simply being passionate about your work.

BREAKTHROUGH TAKEAWAYS

- Don't wait for an external invitation to have your breakthrough. Cultivate your inner authority and call yourself what you are. Start today.
- You don't need to have a huge platform or a huge audience to be relevant. You just need to be able to inspire one person.

It's easy to post an inspirational quote on Facebook. It's not easy to do the work. It's not easy to practice for an entire year. Practice and persistence matter more than simply being passionate about your work.

CHAPTER 12

Find Believers

"Keep away from people who try to belittle your ambitions.
Small people always do that, but the really great ones
make you feel that you too can become great."
—MARK TWAIN

REMEMBER HOW EVAN followed up with me after our conversation on the Santa Monica rooftop? He was in Colorado, and I was in Washington, DC, but that didn't stop him from calling me every week to ask if I'd had "the talk" with my boss yet.

Why did Evan keep calling me? Because I asked him to. I asked him to hold me accountable to what I said I would do. I didn't realize he was actually going to follow through—but that's why finding an accountability partner is so crucial. As soon as you have an idea of what lily pad you want to leap to next, share your idea with people you trust.

When you share your plan with others, you increase your chances of finding supporters who can help you achieve your breakthrough. Remember Cesar, who reached out to me on LinkedIn to get connected to a potential job lead? Or Debbie Sterling, who shared her idea for GoldieBlox with friends, several of whom started working for her? Or Amanda Zimmerman, who reached out to documentary filmmaker Dana Cook, in order to secure a short-term entry-level experience as part of her 4 Months X 4 Cities journey?

Breakthroughs require personal hustle, but they also require outside help. Every breakthrough is the result of both hard work and finding the right people to support your journey. This chapter shares a few ways you can find believers. Building a community of believers is the difference between your breakthrough being a dream and a dream come true.

BUILD YOUR BREAKTHROUGH COMMUNITY

Finding communities of people who share your values and believe in your potential will make your breakthrough possible.

A great example of someone building a supportive community of believers is Jenny Feinberg. Jenny began her career postcollege studying confidence and self-esteem, trying to learn how people gain ambition and what holds many women back from believing in their potential and self-worth. This led Jenny down a path to training women to gain the confidence to run for local political office. She ran Libby Schaaf's first-ever campaign for city council, and four years later, Libby Schaaf became the mayor of Oakland, California.

Jenny learned that running political campaigns is about building trust. She went on to start Makespace, a coworking community, which creates containers of trust and connection among freelancers and creatives. Jenny hosts Makespace pop-up coworking days (and evenings) at cafés, photography studios, restaurants, and offices all around the Bay Area.

While dozens of events and workshops provide programmatic connection, few foster what Jenny calls "a quiet connection." "Our dreams can feel incredibly lonely, isolating, and difficult to sustain because we have no idea where following our intuition may lead us," Jenny says. "I'm running a campaign to sustain San Francisco's creative class so they feel acknowledged and brave. I felt compelled to stand at the forefront of this movement because no one else was advocating for safe and supportive spaces for folks to write, think, and sink into their flow."

Usually, coworking means using your laptop and drinking coffee with other people who are on their laptops and drinking coffee. Not at Makespace. When you attend one of Jenny's Makespace community coworking events, you are introduced to like-minded people, connected to people who are working on similar projects, and offered the ability to share your network and gifts to help others in the community. There's also delicious homemade guacamole and chocolate chip cookies—admittedly, one of the reasons I show up.

"This is the community I've always needed and never had," Jenny explains. "What started as a gut feeling I shared quietly—that others might also struggle to find 'a room of one's own' to consistently (and relentlessly) pursue their dreams—turned into affirming encouragement from the moment I started to share my ideas with others. I wanted these opportunities and experiences to happen more often and more serendipitously, I wanted people to experience a place where permission is assumed and risk taking is the norm."

Makespace is centered around serendipity, what Jenny refers to as the "things that can't be planned." "When you're in a room surrounded by others who've also shown up by choice, there's an inherent magic that will occur," explains Jenny. Makespace is less about networking and more about getting vulnerable. Jenny told me about two Makespace members, Steve and Rachel, who mulled over a start-up idea about health-care access for several months, but came up short on finding real data to support their hypotheses. When discussing these challenges with another Makespacer, it turned out that she was actually working on similar research questions for her consulting firm. She walked Steve and Rachel through the deck she'd just built for her client, and within a few months Steve and Rachel soft launched their new company, Able Health, and raised initial investment. Not long after, Able Health was accepted into Y Combinator, a prestigious accelerator program in Silicon Valley.

If not for this spontaneous interaction with another Makespacer, Steve and Rachel may not have had the confidence to start. Had they been working from a random café, they wouldn't have had the opportunity to share their needs with a stranger. Building your breakthrough community is about finding believers, people who will hold you accountable to your dreams.

WHOM YOU SPEND YOUR TIME WITH MATTERS

The only reason Makespace has been successful thus far is because of the community Jenny built around her. The only reason you're reading this book is because I met people over the past three years who pushed me outside of my comfort zone, encouraged me to take a risk, and held me accountable to do just that. If I hadn't met people like Evan, I would have easily succumbed to the power of naysayers or haters. To be clear, a hater is anyone who keeps you from pursuing your dream. Everyone going through a breakthrough has to face their haters.

Haters can be roommates or good friends—it's unfortunate, but it's true. When I told my roommate back in DC that I wanted to quit my job, he said, "Smiley, suck it up. Everyone hates their job. It's part of life." As I've already mentioned, one of my good friends even told me not to write my book. Can you imagine if I had listened to him?

Who we spend our time with matters. If the people you're currently surrounding yourself with, either at home or at work, aren't helping you get where you need to go, then you need to find some new friends as soon as possible. Supportive or intentional communities can be groups of believers, entrepreneurs, intrapreneurs, innovators, social change makers, coconspirators, artists, teachers, mentors, and friends united in the pursuit of self-empowerment and impact. Your community has your back, makes sure you're following your dreams, and holds you accountable to your goals. Your community allows you to overcome your haters and have a breakthrough.

Depending on what you're interested in and where you live, it might be incredibly easy or rather difficult to find supportive breakthrough communities. Social media may help you find people and groups who are doing things you're excited about, or you may have to reach out to people beyond your network. If you are struggling to find similar communities where you live, use communities like Makespace as inspiration for building your own breakthrough community.

Jenny refers to the Makespace community as her "Quiet Tribe." She explains, "Your Quiet Tribe is a group of ambitious dreamers who know that getting to work is the hardest part of accomplishing our dreams. But it's the only thing that works. Your Quiet Tribe embraces silence as a form of intimacy—holding space instead of always filling it. Your Quiet Tribe holds you accountable to your dreams."

We need to find people who will hold space for us, so we can in turn hold space for others. I often call breakthrough communities, or tribes of believers like Makespace, **exponential communities**, because they have an exponential impact on their members' potential. When Steve and Rachel first joined Makespace, they had nothing but an idea for a start-up. After being part of Makespace, they had a company and had already raised investment capital—they were light-years beyond where they started. When I first went to StartingBloc, I knew I wanted to do something different with my life. After joining StartingBloc, I met people like Evan who would hold me accountable to my new journey as well as people who would support me in writing my first book. *Finding exponential communities is the single most important thing you can do to help your breakthrough.*

Breakthrough Exercise: Find Exponential Communities

Find two to three exponential communities you can join that offer:

- In-person connection
- A chance to meet purpose-driven people who share similar interests
- A safe space to be vulnerable and show up as your full, imperfect self
- Spontaneous interactions and "the things that can't be planned"
- The opportunity to be heard, and the opportunity to listen
- Honest feedback and positive encouragement
- Transformational experiences that take you outside your comfort zone
- Accountability so you can honor your dreams

Social media and sites like Meetup.com can be excellent resources to find such groups. If you're struggling to find exponential communities in your area, try hosting an intentional coworking meet-up yourself, like Jenny's Makespace.

GET VULNERABLE WITH YOUR NEEDS

I used to think that the way to impress people at happy hour was to tell them exactly what they wanted to hear. When I lived in DC and people asked me, "So, what do you do?" I would answer, "I'm working as a special assistant at the Peace Corps, really enjoying it, gaining lots of valuable experience, and this job is a perfect stepping-stone, because I'm thinking about business school next."

To be clear: I used to lie. The truth was I didn't really want to go to business school. I was actually thinking of becoming a freelance writer. I lied because it's a lot easier to pretend you have your life together than to be honest. Being honest can be scary. But people can't help you if they don't know what you need. Every time I told someone that things were going great at work and that I was considering business school next, they said, "Oh, that's wonderful—congrats." The conversation would end, and I'd be left clutching a business card, still knowing in my head that I was screwed.

At the StartingBloc program, after my talk with Evan on the rooftop, I participated in the Ideas Marketplace, where every StartingBloc Fellow pitches an idea for a project or business to the group. Since I didn't have a business to pitch, I decided to get vulnerable and pitch myself. I told the ninety-eight people in the room—most of them strangers—that I was planning on leaving my job that summer to move to San Francisco, and my writing skills were available for anyone who was interested.

Afterward, at least fifteen different people came up to me and connected me with other people interested in writing and social entrepreneurship. One of those people was Nathaniel Koloc, cofounder of ReWork, who was helping Amber Rae launch the Bold Academy in Boulder, Colorado. We stayed in touch after StartingBloc, and I reached out to him about helping out with the first-ever Bold Academy. Nathaniel invited me to volunteer at Bold that summer, and when the company moved to San Francisco, he and Amber offered me the job to be Bold Academy director.

I got that job because I got vulnerable and shared my needs. If I had lied and told everyone at StartingBloc that I didn't need their help and that I was thinking about business school, I would have arrived in San Francisco with nothing but a suitcase after quitting my job. Instead, I arrived with a network of connections and a future job prospect.

Breakthrough Exercise: Sharing Your Needs and Gives

1. Next time you're at a happy hour and someone asks you, *So, what do you do?* be honest. If you're employed and unhappy at your job, say what you'd rather be doing and what you're interested in doing next. If you're unemployed, say you're unemployed and explain what type of job you're looking for.

2. Next time you host or attend a dinner party, let your friends know you want to try something fun. Tell them you're embracing vulnerability by leading this activity. Hand out two sticky notes to each person toward the beginning of the night. On the first one, have everyone list three things they "need" right now, like job leads, fund-raising advice, a creative project to join, or a long hike. On a second sticky note, list three things they're able to "give" the group, like web design help, yoga classes, or cooking someone dinner. After everyone is done, put all the Post-its on the wall in two separate spaces. Have everyone take a look, and see how they can help others, and what they can receive from others in the room.

BREAKTHROUGH VALUES

Not long ago, I got an e-mail from a reader who was struggling to find believers. She asked, "Smiley, how do I know when I've actually found believers? What are the values I should be looking for in my community?" I thought it was an excellent question. Since I had never considered it before, I decided to make a list of the values most common among the believers that have supported my journey so far (some of whom you've read about in this book). Obviously, everyone is different, and you'll have to discover the type of people you want to surround yourself with. Here's what I came up with for the most common values among my believers:

Accountability	Boldness	Love
Vulnerability	Adventurousness	Health
Humility	Positivity	Diversity
Curiosity	Balance	Patience
Learning	Sense of humor	Equality of opportunity
Exploration	Playfulness	Celebrating being weird
Service	Self-actualization	Joy
Compassion	Sustainability	Abundance

IT'S NOT ABOUT YOU; IT'S ABOUT YOUR COMMUNITY

People want to help you. Not in a "like on Facebook" kind of way, in a "like in person" way: they want to help you build your dreams. They want to help you achieve your purpose. But they need to be brought in. They need to be empowered. Give your allies an opportunity to engage with your work, to use their skills and knowledge. Give your community an opportunity to tell you what to do. Listen.

When I launched my first book, I was FREAKING out. I came up with a marketing plan that was a tad ambitious—it had fifty-four different action items on it; one was to get interviewed on NPR! Because my book was about millennials who want to get paid for who they are and the impact they want to make in the world, I figured: what better way to reflect the purpose of my book than to become an entrepreneur myself and crowdsource my book's marketing plan?

So I did something radical: I asked my millennial friends for help. Not in the traditional way an entrepreneur asks for help (*Will you like my Facebook page? Will you buy my book? Will you forward this e-mail to your friends?*), but in a more meaningful way.

I decided to convene the world's first-ever rapid prototyping book marketing event. My friend Matt donated his nonprofit's office space, and twenty-six people showed up on a Saturday afternoon to help me storyboard a book trailer, test memes with quotes from the book, develop my Twitter strategy for the book launch, draft e-mail newsletters for my mailing list, come up with a brilliant way to market my book to parents whose kids are broke and live at home, and figure out how to cross-promote the book with other organizations helping millennials find meaningful work.

Remember, rapid prototyping is about maximizing the rate of learning within time constraints. You'll recall that Tom Chi and his colleagues used rapid prototyping to test their first iteration of Google Glass in less than an hour, and Amanda Zimmerman applied rapid prototyping to her career, testing out four career paths in four different cities, in only four months.

One of the reasons rapid prototyping works is because deadlines matter. Creativity happens when you have to get something done fast. One of the teams at my book marketing event was assigned to make a video trailer for the book. When I came in and saw that they had a storyboard of a trailer for a six-location shoot that would have cost me about $10,000, I told them: "Hey, guys, I want this trailer to be shot and edited in the next fifteen minutes. My budget is zero dollars." You know what happened? They shot and edited the trailer in fifteen minutes.

I learned the valuable lesson that although I spent countless months in the library writing my book and worrying about every single detail of the project, a breakthrough is about releasing control. It's about asking others for their ideas. It's about realizing that you can't do this alone. It's about being honest about your insecurities and imperfections. It's about realizing that you may have some talents, but other people are a lot better than you at most things, and that's totally cool—in fact, that's the point.

A breakthrough is not about how good you are; it's about how strong your community is. Before my rapid prototyping session, I thought my fifty-four-item to-do list was my own, but I learned it was actually a communal to-do list. As my buddy Evan (the same friend who has a weekly ritual to do nothing) reminds me, "Smiley, we have your back. Never forget that we're all in this together." You're never going to get anywhere until you empower your community to help you.

INVEST IN YOUR BREAKTHROUGH COMMUNITY

One Sunday evening when I lived in DC, I was sitting on a park bench with my friend Meredith. I was telling her how much I was dreading going to work the next day. She was also feeling bored at work, and she told me about a social innovation fellowship program called StartingBloc she had recently applied to. The program brought together motivated young professionals interested in changing the world, and the deadline for the next institute was that night at midnight! I rushed home to fill out the application.

A couple of months later, when I found out I had been accepted to the program, I began to get really excited, until I realized it cost $1,000. I thought to myself: I'm considering leaving my job; I can't afford to waste $1,000 right now. Meredith was also nervous to spend that much money, but we both finally decided it was probably worth spending the money on our careers, as opposed to food or booze.

That $1,000 was the best money I've ever spent. I met nearly a hundred people who became enthusiastic supporters of my breakthrough. They started following my blog, connected me to other writers and social entrepreneurs in San Francisco, and provided the net I needed to catch me when I leapt. After the program ended, I found writing opportunities through our group's Facebook page, including interviewing entrepreneurs for the StartSomeGood blog, editing a book, and writing guest posts for a social-impact blog, which led to my getting published in *Forbes*.

Investing in your breakthrough doesn't mean you have to spend a ton of money (especially if you're low on savings)—you can also invest your *time*. Remember how I met Nathaniel, ReWork's cofounder, and he asked me to come volunteer at the first Bold Academy? I could have easily turned down the experience because it was unpaid. But I decided volunteering at Bold would be a worthwhile investment of my *time*. In eight days, I met fifteen inspiring young leaders, and numerous staff and mentors, including people who worked at TED, IDEO, and the Unreasonable Institute. Because I was an engaged volunteer, Amber Rae, the CEO of Bold Academy, reached out and asked me if I'd be interested in running their next program. At Bold Academy, I got introduced to Ryan Allis, who later launched the Hive Global Leaders Program, which I also ended up working for.

So, for the cost of going to StartingBloc, then giving eight days of my time at Bold Academy, I got inspired to have my breakthrough, met several now-close friends, published numerous pieces, and got two paying jobs allowing me to share my gifts with the world. Was the investment of time and resources worth it? I definitely think so.

Below are several investments in your breakthrough community that offer a high return on investment. While a graduate studies program can certainly be a worthwhile breakthrough investment depending on your long-term goals, the exorbitant cost makes it a lot riskier.

BREAKTHROUGH INVESTMENTS WITH HIGH ROI

1. Attend a leadership development program or apply for a fellowship program that aligns with one of your current interests. (Note: many of these programs have scholarships available if you need financial assistance.)

2. Attend a conference or event that interests you, like a trade summit, start-up weekend, film festival, maker fair, craft fair, or political conference. (Note: some of these events can be expensive. See if they have a volunteer application—that way you can attend and meet interesting people *for free*.)

3. Enroll in a class or workshop for a skill you want to develop. The class could be online or in person, and there are plenty of great ones offered through General Assembly, Skillshare, and Udemy, to name a few.
4. Offer your time. Find a short-term apprenticeship, internship, or volunteer opportunity that allows you to meet people, gain experience, and further your breakthrough goals.

CREATE A BREAKTHROUGH ADVISORY TEAM

After I finally had "the talk" with my boss, I assembled a small team of mentors, friends, and strangers to support me during the months leading up to my last day at work.

Whenever I started getting nervous about my upcoming transition, I knew I could reach out to my team for guidance. I selected advisors with experience in the areas I wanted to work in, as well as ones based in San Francisco, which meant that these people were also helping me network for future opportunities. I also selected two members that I had never met before, reaching beyond my immediate contacts and expanding my network.

Be selective when assembling your advisory team. Remember: people can only give the advice they know how to give. If you want to pursue a new path, find someone who has experience in that area and who works for the type of organization you want to work for. Deepa was able to find people in a sector where she had few contacts by starting to hang out with people who worked in social impact instead of tech.

You may need to spend some time (after your one-week social media sabbatical) using social media or relevant websites and blogs to find suitable members for your breakthrough advisory team. The search process will help you identify people who share your values and can get you to the next lily pad. Think of your team like an organization thinks of their board of advisors: the stronger the board, the better the performance of the organization.

REMEMBER TO PLAY

Keep in mind that breakthrough communities don't have to be strictly professional in nature—breakthrough communities are about having fun, not simply networking—the important thing is to find people who will hold space for you and have your back. The important thing is to find a community of people who are dedicated to something greater than themselves.

Breakthrough communities are the only reason I've been able to take steps toward my potential in the last three years. In San Francisco, in addition to my supportive coworking community at Makespace, I'm part of Jessica Seeman's Passion Co. community, a group of people who support each other in completing a thirty-day passion project. Since I love to eat, I'm part of the Real Food Real Stories community, a gathering of people interested in supporting local food producers and hearing the personal stories behind why people make food.

I'm also part of the Digital Detox community, which believes that it's important to step away from technology and play. I've been a counselor for Camp Grounded, Digital Detox's tech-free summer camp for adults in the redwoods, ten times. At Camp Grounded, I always meet tons of interesting people, all because we share an interest in *Wet Hot American Summer*, camp crushes, embracing our inner child, stargazing, and spending a weekend without Facebook and Instagram.

At Camp Grounded, we don't use digital technology, we don't talk about work, we don't talk about age, we don't use drugs or alcohol, and we call people by camp nicknames instead of their real names. At camp, we believe that play is just as important for adults as it is for kids. As someone who spends too much of my life on my digital devices, I learn a lot more from watching three hundred adults with nicknames like Honey Bear, Popcorn, Bubbles, Hungarian Sheep Dog, Dolphin, Smooth Operator, and Tiny Dancer become their best selves than I could ever learn from checking my Facebook feed thirty times a day. Here are a few life lessons learned at summer camp that I'm trying to incorporate back into my technology-prone daily life in San Francisco.

1. Take time to take time

We're always moving, we're always going somewhere, we're always doing something, we're always busy. We're busy being busy, but we're rarely busy just being. At camp, I spend a lot of time relaxing in nature. I spend a lot of time doing nothing, and in turn, seeing everything: The late-afternoon sunlight pouring through the redwoods making my eyes squint and my heart expand. The luminous moon smiling down from her throne. The birds chirping love songs to each other. The ice-cold river passing over my feet. The ding a typewriter makes when you finish typing a line, as if to say, *Keep typing, you incredible warrior, keep typing!*

Take time—especially in the moments when you are alone—to breathe. To look at the world around you, instead of your phone. It's these moments when you have nothing to do—when you're waiting for the bus or in line to buy a cup of coffee—when time sort of stops and says, *Well, you're alone now, this is kind of awkward, I guess you should check Instagram*—that make up much of our lives. When you take time to take time, you remember why you're here.

2. Make eye contact

The default way of talking to someone is to look past them and scan the room for someone more interesting, successful, or attractive. This is rude. It's also unwise since each person we meet may share wisdom that inspires us or changes our perspective on life. When you make eye contact, you are actually listening to someone—you are validating their reason for being and they in turn will value yours. When you look down at your phone when you meet someone, you are communicating that the Gmail notification you just received (alerting you that your Bank of America statement is now available online) is more important than a human being's heart. Always remember to like people in person. Treat others like they're a beautiful person who has something precious to teach you—because they most definitely are.

3. Your job (however cool or not) does not define you

Society likes to box people by their name or ethnicity or where they live or what they do or how much money they make. A person is not a box to be checked off in an annual census. A person cannot be defined by labels or prejudices or guesses or judgments. At Camp Grounded we don't call people by their real names, and we don't talk about what they do for work. So when you meet Uncle Freckles, you are not thinking, Oh, he works at Google, he must be like so and so, or She runs a nonprofit, she must be like so and so, or She's unemployed and broke and lives with her parents, she must be like so and so.

Starting a conversation with *What do you do?* is a good way to ensure the conversation will be as boring as every other conversation you normally have at happy hour. At camp we ask things like, *What's your spirit animal?* or *If I were to go traveling with you, where would we go?* or *What's a fear you want to overcome?* Beyond just asking questions, you have to listen to others, and realize that getting to know someone has nothing to do with their job title. Greatness is rarely found on a résumé; greatness is experienced when we allow people to share their gifts. Gifts can be anything from the way someone hugs to the way they write a poem to the way they dance to the way they listen. Gifts let us see how infinite someone is, which makes us feel infinite, too.

4. Your age (however young or old) does not define you

At Camp Grounded, we don't judge someone based on their age, we judge someone on how much they love to play. Play reminds us that age is irrelevant. Anyone can play. I have met a camper over the age of seventy who can build the most epic sandcastle you've ever seen, a camper over the age of forty who frees the jail four times during Capture the Flag, and a camper in his twenties who didn't sleep much at camp because he was having too much fun, despite the fact that he was also fighting cancer. Just because you know someone's age doesn't mean you know what's going on in their life.

5. Validation is power

The role of a camp counselor—similar to that of a teacher, coach, or mentor—is largely undervalued in our society. The role of a camp counselor is to validate their campers. To tell their camper: *You are okay exactly the way you are, you are awesome, you belong.* We don't get told that enough as kids, and we certainly don't get told that enough as adults. Rather, we get told things like, *You're not smart enough, you need to get better at math, you need to dress sexier, you need to lose weight, you need to stop being so weird, you need to stop playing, you need to stop making so much noise, you need to pay better attention, you need to buy more of what I'm selling, you need to make more money, you need to change your life, you need to change your life NOW!*

The truth is people just don't need to change as much as they need to be validated for who they really are. When everyone is given permission to be themselves, everyone is imperfect, which is to say, everyone is perfect. You can have a profound impact on the world simply by turning whatever environment you spend your days in—be it an office, a school, or a camp in the woods—into a place where everyone feels validated. When we create this kind of community, when everyone belongs, people are empowered to fully express themselves and anything is possible.

TAKE YOUR FRIENDS SERIOUSLY

Building your breakthrough community, just like being a camp counselor, starts with how you show up for the people around you.

Recently, one of my best friends started a podcast called BizzleCast. On BizzleCast, Jesse (aka, the Bizzle) embraces his inner-nerd and hosts hour-long (actually, two- or three-hour-long) podcasts about his love for movies like *Star Wars*, *The Matrix*, the Lord of the Rings trilogy, *Guardians of the Galaxy*, and *Deadpool*. Jesse recently recorded his own audio commentary for all three extended-edition Lord of the Rings films—*The Fellowship of the Ring*, *The Two Towers*, and *The Return of the King*—which, in total, lasts eleven hours.

Another friend and I were having a conversation about BizzleCast, and my friend joked, "Who the hell is going to listen to Jesse wax poetic for eleven hours about Gandalf? What a dork! That dude is wasting his time!"

At first, I started laughing. But then I realized that if I was laughing at Jesse for creating something he cared about, something that was truly and authentically his own, then how was that any different from people laughing at me when I told them I was going to write a book? How was it any different from my buddy telling me that I shouldn't write a book, that my book had already been written hundreds of times, by people a lot smarter than me?

In less than a year, BizzleCast has been listened to more than five thousand times, and in addition to fantasy movies, Jesse has explored topics like the modern-day relevance of Taoism, how Muslims triumphed in medieval Spain, and the impact of misogyny in sports culture. Several BizzleCast podcasts reference academic research he did while studying for his master's in religious studies at Temple University, and he's using these episodes as supplemental material as he applies for new teaching jobs. BizzleCast has also inspired Jesse to start writing his first fantasy sci-fi novel, called *The Book of Korba*.

It's easy to make fun of your friends and come up with twenty reasons why they shouldn't do something. I have a feeling that when J. R. R. Tolkien had a beer with his buddies and told them that he was creating a world called Middle Earth, they probably looked at him like he was insane and said, *Yeah, okaaaay, man. You're a huge nerd. You're just wasting your time.*

It's a lot harder to take your friends seriously. If your friend is pursuing something that makes them come alive, encourage them to keep going—even if that thing is Han Solo or Gandalf. Your friend's curiosity, your friend's inner nerd, might be the very thing that provides meaning in their lives and leads to their breakthrough. As Tolkien once wrote, "Not all those who wander are lost."

CELEBRATE YOUR FRIENDS

Earlier, I shared how Facebook-induced FOMO nearly crippled me during my quarter-life crisis. I was paying so much attention to the lily pads my friends were jumping to that I barely could hear what my own heart was saying. I wish I could report that FOMO goes away once you've had a breakthrough, but it really never does.

Last year, I felt really proud of my accomplishments: I had a book deal and was getting paid to speak to audiences around the world—how awesome is that? Then, I would go on Facebook and see, in succession, posts similar to these:

- "So proud of my friend for her company being named the most innovative medical start-up of the year!"
- "Last day in Brazil soaking up the sun and 80-degree perfect weather with my beautiful love. I love my life! #vacation #bliss #engaged"
- "Flying to Austin for SXSW tomorrow. This year, I'm not only performing in the music festival, my documentary is being featured!"
- "I'm off to Uganda to change the world!"
- "Honored to be included in the *Forbes* 30 Under 30 for social entrepreneurs. What an incredible group."
- "So this happened. I just raised $10 million! I. Can't. Even."

How is it possible to stay confident in your life decisions when your friends are doing such amazing things? You could literally be in the most beautiful place on Earth, doing the most meaningful thing on Earth, kissing the most beautiful person on Earth, and your Instagram feed would still make you say, *Hmmm, I wish I were doing that.*

I don't have an answer to this conundrum. Your friends are always going to be doing amazing things. You could always be doing something else, somewhere more beautiful. This is a fact of life. My advice is to prioritize your unique contribution. Worry less about what others are doing and more about why you're here. I also believe that Facebook-induced FOMO and jealousy have the potential to paralyze our generation, and that if we really want to thrive, we have to celebrate our friends' accomplishments.

So when you see a friend's Facebook post that induces equal parts inspiration and envy, consider how hard your friend worked to achieve their accomplishment. Celebrate your friends. Share their posts. Feel joy not just when you win something, but when your community wins something. Remember, *a breakthrough is not about how good you are; it's about how strong your community is.* Ask yourself: How can you support your friend's breakthrough? Do you know someone working on a similar project who your friend should meet? Do you have access to funding or opportunities that can help your friend's breakthrough?

Our generation faces an endless slew of challenges, and the only way we're going to solve them is when we move from envy to joy, from competition to collaboration, when we support each other's dreams to change the world.

BREAKTHROUGH TAKEAWAYS

- Finding communities of people who share your values and believe in your potential will make your breakthrough possible. Exponential communities have an exponential impact on their members' potential.
- Whom you spend your time with matters. If the people you're currently surrounding yourself with, either at home or at work, aren't helping you get where you need to go, then you need to find some new friends as soon as possible. When you find those friends, take them seriously and celebrate their accomplishments.

An investment in your breakthrough community is the best possible use of your time and resources.

CHAPTER 13

Leave a Legacy

*"There is no passion to be found playing small—in settling for a
life that is less than the one you are capable of living."*
—NELSON MANDELA

THE MILLENNIALS YOU'VE READ about in this book changed my life. They're the only reason I'm living in a city I love, spending my days doing something that energizes me, dedicating my life to empowering others to find meaning. They're the only reason I'm not sitting at home, depressed, spending my days scrolling through Facebook, worrying about what all my friends are doing, jealous of my friend the baller corporate lawyer (who doesn't even want to be a corporate lawyer!).

When you pursue meaningful work, you inspire others to as well. You ensure that the workforce of the future will be spending its days empowering girls to become engineers, teaching financial literacy and entrepreneurship to urban youth, employing people with disabilities, and ensuring that every single person—regardless of where they are born—reaches their full potential.

Having a breakthrough is about leaving behind something for others; it's about creating a legacy. Your legacy is how people will remember you, beyond your twenties, and after your life. While we should all be so lucky to find work that matters, the final story I'll share reminds us that there is nothing more powerful than helping *others* make their dreams a reality.

PASS THE TORCH

Syreeta Gates started selling popcorn to her classmates in the fourth grade to make some extra cash, and she's been hustling ever since. She graduated to selling bookmarks and cupcakes, and in high school sold T-shirts and two-way pagers. Her entrepreneurial efforts showed her the importance of relationships at an early age. "My mom told me to be mindful of who you are in the world, because people are always watching," remembers Syreeta.

Growing up in Jamaica, Queens, Syreeta's uncles taught her about hip-hop culture, exposing her to graffiti, beatboxing, break dancing, and emceeing. Hip-hop became a way of life for Syreeta; it enabled her to understand the cultural diversity of her community, learn her family's history, and explore her life purpose. She saw hip-hop as a way to bridge generations, discovering the historical parallels between her grandmother—who grew up in the 1920s and moved from North Carolina to Harlem as part of the Great Migration of blacks from the rural South; her mother—who was born in 1950 in the era of the Black Arts Movement, a group of politically motivated artists that grew out of the Black Power movement; and her uncles—who were teenagers in Queens in the 1980s and couldn't stop watching *Wild Style*, and when they got older, drove around blasting EPMD, Nas, Biggie, and Wu-Tang Clan.

Syreeta's passion for hip-hop history led to her getting featured on New York's popular morning radio show *Wake Up Call* with Esther Armah, on WBAI. She went on to become editor in chief of *Carter*, a hip-hop magazine, and become the first person ever to earn a degree in urban youth culture from Hunter College. Syreeta is now using hip-hop to educate and inspire young people in the same city where she grew up. "Any topic can be linked to hip-hop," Syreeta explains. "If I want the kids to get excited about science, I use references to Wu-Tang Clan lyrics. If we're doing a lesson about food, I'll cite rapper Action Bronson. If it's finance, we'll listen to Jay-Z, who raps about Goldman Sachs. If we're discussing the importance of knowledge and consciousness, I'll play Lupe Fiasco, who talks about Dr. Cornel West."

Syreeta is a dream director for the Future Project, a nonprofit that helps young people realize their infinite possibilities and live extraordinary lives of passion and purpose. Since 2011, the Future Project has placed dream directors in schools in New York City, Washington, DC, Detroit, Newark,

New Haven, and San Francisco, helping over twenty-five thousand students take action toward their dreams. Syreeta worked out of August Martin High School in Queens, one of the least popular high schools in all of New York City, with historically low attendance and graduation rates. "When an entire generation is deemed 'at-risk,' you disempower us. And then the world is at risk of missing out on the next movement driven by us," says Syreeta.

Syreeta empowers her high school students, most of whom have grown up with little access or opportunity, by doing something quite simple: actually believing in them. She tells her students to be great, to go make it happen, to do things that they've never done before. She helped her "dream team" of thirty ninth to twelfth graders come up with Operation Skittles, a group project to transform the hallways of the school from institutional white walls that made the students feel like they were inside an insane asylum, into a colorful graffiti mecca. The students had to complete surveys to figure out what the other students wanted, pitch the project to the principal, pitch the project to other students, learn how to make the ask, get used to hearing "no," and appreciate when teachers and students said "yes."

Operation Skittles taught the students important business skills in research, writing, public speaking, fund-raising, creating a budget, and getting press coverage from media outlets like CBS. The hallway now features world-class graffiti art from Five Pointz, a Queens-based graffiti collective, and inspirational quotes from people like Russell Simmons, Kid President, Gandhi, Rosa Clemente, and Che Guevara. Some of the graffiti artists traveled from as far away as Japan and France to donate their work. Many of the students now feel like August Martin is a cool place they want to be, and that they actually have a voice at the school.

"I rock with young people by letting them take the lead," Syreeta explains. "I have them do the work. They learn by making it happen. I'm not from a privileged background—I learned by creating things that didn't exist. My grandmother taught me that I might not have money, but I might know someone who has access to the thing I want to buy. That access is power."

Syreeta has found alignment between who she is, what her interests and talents are, how she spends her days, how she makes a living, and the people she surrounds herself with. She gets meaning from making her community better.

I think life's most beautiful blessing is to be able to spend your days feeling alive, while making others come alive as well. How will you share your knowledge with your community? How will you pass the torch? How will you build a career worth having?

KNOW WHAT IS ENOUGH

Remember Dorothy, the management consultant turned career coach for MBAs? In our interview, I asked Dorothy, how do you know what is "enough" in terms of salary or impact? How do you know when you can be satisfied? How do you know when you've achieved your mission?

Twentysomethings rarely get asked this question. The whole point of being in your twenties, the whole point of youth, is to *not be satisfied*. The goal is to question, to explore, to experiment, to learn, to challenge ourselves and hustle toward something more: more impact, more meaning, more, more, more. Yet I've noticed that people I meet, young and old, who say they are fulfilled, do know what is enough. This doesn't mean they stop striving or hustling, but they are able to step back and know that they've accomplished something in this life worth accomplishing. They know what it feels like to be content. They know the legacy they're leaving behind.

Dorothy told me something that struck me as essential when thinking about legacy. "I am satisfied today," she said. "If I died today, I would have no regret in how I impacted others and how I lived from day to day. That doesn't mean I won't keep working. I will have goals, both financial and work-related. But today is also enough."

Having an appreciation for your life *today* is incredibly powerful. I've experienced this contentment only in the past year of my life. If someone had asked me several years ago, when I was twenty-eight and working for the Peace Corps, if my life was enough, I would have probably said no. I would have felt like I wasn't doing what I was meant to be doing. I would have felt like something was incomplete for me, that I hadn't achieved what I was truly capable of achieving, that I hadn't reached my full potential.

If you asked me that question today, I'd say that what I have right now is enough. I have the beautiful opportunity to help people with my words, and that is enough. When I receive an e-mail from a young reader like Amanda who tells me my book inspired her 4 Months X 4 Cities journey, it is enough. When I receive a tweet that says, "Not even halfway through your book and my life is already changing drastically," it is enough. When I run into someone who tells me my talk (in front of four people in the lobby of an office building) inspired her to quit her job and start a new career, it is enough. When one of my campers at Camp Grounded says to me, "Smiley, playing games with you has made me feel more alive than I've felt in twenty years," it is enough.

At the same time I get these messages, I'm living with five roommates in an apartment with ants and mice, and freaking out about how I'm going to afford to survive as a writer in San Francisco and raise a family one day. I still spend thirty minutes before going on a date obsessing about whether it's okay for me to wear running shoes. But I also know that the meaning I've already experienced is enough. I know that tomorrow, if a great earthquake swallowed San Francisco, or my arch nemesis King Joffrey were to capture me and chop off my head like I was Ned Stark in *Game of Thrones* (long live Winterfell!), I would be okay. I would not have any regrets.

Don't get me wrong: I have no plans to go any time soon. I'm not done writing, I'm not done speaking, I'm not done building communities of change makers, and I'm certainly not done eating bagels with lox and cream cheese. I plan on being Smiley for long enough to write *The Midlife Breakthrough*, and hopefully long enough to write *The Retirement Breakthrough* as well. But I know what is enough to make me satisfied, to make me complete, to make me whole, today, not tomorrow.

There's no road map for how to get there, but if we can get to the place where Dorothy got to, where *today is enough*, well, then that seems as worthy a goal for life as any.

Do you know what is enough? Do you know what your legacy will be?

KEEP GOING

Over the past few years, I jumped headfirst into the creative vortex and somehow made it to the other side. The creative vortex is what separates the *I want to create* from the *I did create*, the idea from the doing of the idea. For me, this meant going from what was once a far-fetched dream to write a book, to actually writing the book, to pressing "send" to a publisher in New York City.

Not a day has gone by in the last three years where I haven't had to balance the voice inside my heart telling me to keep going with the far more practical voice inside my head telling me to be realistic and go get a real job. Sometimes the practical voice gets so loud that I can't even hear myself think, and I start e-mailing every single person I know who works for a tech company that gives out free snacks, to see if they are hiring.

Learning to balance this tension between the fire that burns within your heart and the practical voice inside your head is what makes you a breakthrough hustler. It's what allows you to make the hardest decision you ever have to make (which you have to make every single day— sometimes two or three times a day): *the decision to keep going.* To not get distracted by projects that may fulfill other people's agendas, but not your own. To realize that if you are going to work in alignment with your purpose, if you are going to believe in yourself, then there is no end date or finish line.

I wish I could tell you that practical voice goes away, but it doesn't. But at some point you realize that the very instincts telling you to hold back are the same fears that inspired you to jump into the creative vortex in the first place.

When the first edition of my book came out, most of the reviews were very positive. Of course, I had critics—everyone has critics. One reader wrote, "Not for everybody. [This is] the definitive guide to slicing your income in half, moving to San Fran, and transforming into a smug, self-satisfied hipster." This particular review made me laugh, because it's rather astute. I did in fact cut my income in half (by choice, of course), move to San Francisco, and start drinking lots of kombucha—I've always kind of been a self-satisfied hipster.

You have to be willing to take criticism and use it as fuel to make you work harder. To stop receiving criticism is to stop creating. Not everyone is going to love what you do, and that's perfectly okay. The point is not to be loved, it's to make your unique contribution.

The reality is that jumping into the creative vortex, while seemingly impossible, is actually the easy part. The process of sharing your work, of struggling to sustain your work, of building a supportive community for your work, is far harder and scarier than conceiving it in the first place. I now know that day 1,095 requires far more dedication than day one, but I also know that day 1,095 is a lot more meaningful than day one. As Viktor Frankl wrote in *Man's Search for Meaning*, "What man actually needs is not a tensionless state but rather the striving and struggling for some goal worthy of him. What he needs is not the discharge of tension at any cost, but the call of a potential meaning waiting to be fulfilled by him."

Each of the twenty- and thirtysomethings profiled in this book are drastically different, but they share one important thing in common: they've refused to settle for mediocre work. Instead, they've decided to spend their days doing something that inspires them, something that makes an impact they're uniquely capable of making. Their stories prove that you too can get paid to be who you are, you can get paid to follow your dreams, and you can get paid to make a positive impact in the world. Meaning is possible, if you're willing to work for it.

If you take your breakthrough seriously enough to take action, and hustle to make your dreams for working with purpose a reality, you can't fail.

BREAKTHROUGH TAKEAWAYS

- Having a breakthrough is about leaving behind something for others; it's about creating a legacy. Your legacy is how people will remember you, beyond your twenties, and after your life.
- Having an appreciation for your life *today* is incredibly powerful. People who are fulfilled know what is enough. They are able to step back and know that they've accomplished something in this life worth accomplishing.

The hardest decision you ever have to make is *the decision to keep going*. Not everyone is going to love what you do, and that's perfectly okay. The point is not to be loved, it's to make your unique contribution.

The Journey Continues

"This is the true joy in life, the being used for a purpose
recognized by yourself as a mighty one."
—GEORGE BERNARD SHAW

SEVERAL YEARS AGO, my mom retired as a federal employee, having worked for over thirty years as a nurse practitioner at the Veterans Administration (VA) in Boston. Most of her patients were World War II and Vietnam War veterans, and in recent years, she specialized in hospice and palliative care, improving end-of-life care for veterans and their families.

I asked my mom what her thoughts were about retirement. Despite her long hours, the stress of working with patients suffering from PTSD, and the challenges of the VA's cumbersome bureaucracy, she told me she was leaving the best job of her life. She said, "It was an enormous privilege to provide comfort for people at a very vulnerable time in their lives—to help relieve their pain and suffering. I feel so truly lucky to have found a career that gave me so much."

Far from a retirement mind-set, where she was counting down the days until she could leave her job, the work had been so meaningful to her that after some well-deserved time off, my mom leapt to another lily pad, and is now working as a hospice volunteer. Whether we have the same employer for over thirty years, or eight different jobs between the ages of twenty-two and thirty, we should all be so blessed to find work that moves us and makes a lasting impact in others' lives.

With a retirement mind-set, we work our whole lives in order to spend a few years post-sixty-five playing golf. With a lily pad career mind-set, we spend our whole lives doing something that matters—our work is so purposeful that when we turn sixty-five, we can't even bring ourselves to stop working (and we certainly don't have any reason to play golf).

It's hard to say where each of the breakthrough hustlers you met in this book will be in a year, let alone five years. But by taking their breakthroughs seriously, each got closer to redefining success on their own terms. Success is not a front-page news story, a huge paycheck, a venture capital investment, or climbing to the top of a ladder. Success doesn't mean knowing all the answers. Instead, it's starting to ask the right questions. *Success is embracing the journey to get closer to what you want to give to the world.*

Jumping lily pads, listening to my heart, and beginning my career as a writer and public speaker has made the last three years the most meaningful of my life, exposed me to the inspiring people and experiences you read about in this book, and brought me one step closer to the impact I want to have on this world. Refusing to settle and embracing the journey to find meaningful work has helped me discover *why* I'm here—and where I'm going.

The journey to find meaningful work never really ends. In two or five or ten years, you may find yourself bored at work or unemployed, living at the intersection of hopeless, stuck, and FOMO, and in a similar position you were in when you began this book. And that's to be expected. If the voice goes off in your head alerting you to the fact that something's not working, *listen.* Get clarity on how you want to share your gifts, and hustle to your next lily pad.

I don't know the exact age when the "quarter-life breakthrough" becomes the "midlife breakthrough," but I'll let you know when I find out for sure—that will be part of the sequel! You're never too old to have a breakthrough. It's never too late to ask *why?*, and it's always a good time to flip back to the first page of this book.

I hope your quarter-life breakthrough, and the next one, and the next, bring you closer to who you are, the types of people and experiences that make you come alive, and the change you want for the world. I can't wait to see the legacy you leave behind as you build a life that matters.

Join the Breakthrough Community

QUARTER-LIFE BREAKTHROUGHS ARE contagious. Please consider sharing the story of your breakthrough with your friends and community, as a way of sharing the love and encouraging your peers to pursue meaningful work. There are a number of easy ways to do this:

1. Gift this book to a friend or stranger who needs to read it.
2. Write a blog post about your breakthrough.
3. Instagram a selfie of you reading the book (#QuarterLifeBreakthrough).
4. Talk about your breakthrough with your friends, family, and coworkers.
5. Host a #QuarterLifeBreakthrough-themed dinner party at your house: make vision boards, have your friends fill out their Breakthrough Goal Maps, and lead a Needs and Gives exercise!
6. Use the Resources (including the end notes and sources used in writing this book) available at smileyposwolsky.com.

I encourage you to reach out to your fellow breakthrough hustlers for mutual support. I'd love to hear about your own journey, too. **E-mail** smiley@thequarterlifebreakthrough.com, or say what's up in any of these places:

Web smileyposwolsky.com
Facebook The Quarter-Life Breakthrough
Twitter/Instagram @whatsupsmiley
LinkedIn Adam Smiley Poswolsky

Gratitude

THIS BOOK WOULD not be possible without the brave twenty- and thirty-somethings who inspired this project and shared their stories with me. To all of the breakthrough hustlers featured in this book: thank you for being vulnerable, thank you for refusing to settle, thank you for being you.

To Lisa Tauber: thank you for meeting with me back in 2013, and for introducing me to the best agent an author could ask for. To my agent, Lindsay Edgecombe, and the entire team at Levine Greenberg Rostan: I feel so lucky to be represented by someone who believes in both my writing and my mission. Lindsay: thank you for advising me every step (freak-out) of the way, and being a true mentor and friend.

To my talented editor, Jeanette Shaw: thank you for believing in this project from our very first phone call. Working with you was a joy; this book is infinitely better than what we started with. To Joel Fotinos, John Duff, Jessica Morphew, Katy Riegel, Zoe Norvell, Keely Platte, and everyone at TarcherPerigee and Penguin Random House: thanks for making this book come to life.

I am indebted to everyone who believed in this project three years ago, when I had nothing but a dream to write a book. Thank you for reading my early blog posts and encouraging me to keep going. To the 518 people in thirty-eight countries who supported my Indiegogo campaign: thank you for empowering this dream. This book exists because of you. A special thank-you to Caroline Kessler for editing the first edition. Thanks to Sumeet Banerji, Bernat Fortet Unanue, and Kara Brodgesell, for your work on the self-published edition.

I want to express love and gratitude to all of the breakthrough communities that have made me come alive. To my Hive family: thank you for your commitment to what the world needs most. To my Camp Grounded family: thank you for reminding me to turn off my phone and play. To my Passion Co. family: thank you for supporting this project when it was just getting off the ground. To my Makespace family: thank you for providing my creative home in San Francisco. To my StartingBloc family, all over the world: thank you for waking me up, thank you for changing my life. To my Bold Academy family: thank you for the tiny piece of chalk that eventually led to this book.

To my Peace Corps family: thank you for your incredible service, and for teaching me what it really means to make an impact.

To my Wesleyan family and the Ruby crew: thank you for teaching me how to have fun. I may not have learned how to find a job in college, but I sure learned how to find friends that make me happy, which is a tad more important. Thank you to my beautiful friends and mentors who remind me what matters most in life, especially: Andreas Mendez-Peñate, Jesse Brenner, Gabriel Prager, Kevin Haas, Zeb Zankel, Philip Amidon, Ryan Goldberg, Satya Kamdar, Levi Felix, Brooke Dean, Brady Gil, Christine Lai, Evan Kleiman, Evan Walden, Nathaniel Koloc, Dev Aujla, Antonio Neves, Sydney Malawer, Jenny Feinberg, Amber Rae, Ben Tseitlin, Jessica Semaan, Nate Bagley, Kelly McFarling, and my roommates past and present.

Most important, thank you to my family. Mom and Dad: thank you for believing in me when I told you I wanted to be Mister Rogers, play for the Red Sox, be a filmmaker, be a writer, and for believing in whatever it is I tell you I want to be next. Becca: you inspire me to stay true to myself; I love you more than the world. Gran and Grandma: thank you for teaching me how to laugh; I miss you every single day.

Thank you to everyone who has carried me on my journey thus far, from Cambridge, to Middletown, to Brooklyn, to Buenos Aires, to Indiana, to DC, to San Francisco. You know who you are. I love you and am forever grateful.

Bonus Gift

In order to help your breakthrough, I've created several free bonus materials. Go to *smileyposwolsky.com/bonus* to receive your gift:

- A printable Quarter-Life Breakthrough poster with exercises from the book.
- A Breakthrough Goal Map so you can print extra copies for your friends!
- An updated Quarter-Life Breakthrough Career Resources Guide

About the Author

Jayson Carpenter

ADAM SMILEY POSWOLSKY is a millennial career expert who has inspired thousands of young professionals and entrepreneurs to find fulfilling work. Smiley is the founding director of community engagement for the Hive Global Leaders Program, former director of the Bold Academy, mentor for the StartingBloc Institute for Social Innovation, and an instructor for General Assembly and the Passion Co. He is also a ten-time counselor for Camp Grounded, a summer camp for adults where grown-ups go to unplug and be kids again.

An internationally renowned motivational speaker, Smiley speaks about finding meaningful work at Fortune 500 companies, TEDx events, business conferences, leadership development programs, and colleges and graduate schools. Smiley writes stories about purpose-driven millennials who are making a positive impact in their communities. His writing has been published in *The Washington Post*, *Fast Company*, and *GOOD*, among others. He previously worked as special assistant to the director of global operations at the US Peace Corps.

He is a proud graduate of Wesleyan University and can often be found dancing in San Francisco, California.

@whatsupsmiley #QuarterLifeBreakthrough
smileyposwolsky.com

Smiley is available for career workshops and speaking engagements.
To inquire, please visit *smileyposwolsky.com/speaking*.